LETTERS AND SOUNDS:
A manual for reading instruction

Robert E. Schell

Letters and Sounds: A Manual for Reading Instruction by Robert E. Schell guides the teacher or parent to improve a child's reading skill in a matter of days. The book shows how to instruct and how to understand the nature and goals of reading.

This manual is a comprehensive introduction to the elements of reading instruction. The unique feature is the concentration on **all** of the sound-letter relationships required to read American English. These relationships are presented step-by-step, with frequent illustrations, examples, and suggestions. An easy-to-follow style adds to the book's clarity and usefulness.

There is no other book quite as flexible or even fully comparable to **Letters and Sounds: A Manual for Reading Instruction.** It is based on present research and offers sensible approaches to the uses and applications of sounds in the teaching of reading. The summary information on sound-letter relations has not yet appeared in any other book. It is well organized with tabs and indexes to be consulted much like a dictionary. Such convenience permits the book to be used for a variety of reading purposes including related spelling activities.

The realistic approach makes this book an effective teaching aid regardless of a person's background, interest, or level of skill. It has been tested with both children and illiterate adults, and found to

and Acting Director, Psychological Clinic, Michigan State University; Associate Professor, Psychology Department, Dartmouth.

LETTERS

AND

SOUNDS

LETTERS AND SOUNDS

A Manual for Reading Instruction

ROBERT E. SCHELL

PRENTICE-HALL, INC.

Englewood Cliffs, New Jersey

10 9 8 7 6 5 4 3 2 1

ISBN: P 0-13-531939-0

C 0-13-531947-1

Library of Congress Catalog Card Number: 74-168758

Printed in the United States of America

Prentice-Hall International, Inc., *London*
Prentice-Hall of Australia, Pty. Ltd., *Sydney*
Prentice-Hall of Canada, Ltd., *Toronto*
Prentice-Hall of India Private Limited, *New Delhi*
Prentice-Hall of Japan, Inc., *Tokyo*

To facilitate use of this text, an index tab on the first page of each new section has been aligned with the corresponding letter in the master index on this page. To use the index, bend the pages of the book back until the tabs appear; use the master index presented here to select the section you desire.

L-S
RR
SR
WL
I
II
III
IV
V
VI
VII
VIII
IX
X
XI
XII
XIII
XIV
XV
XVI
XVII
XVIII
XIX
XX
XXI
APP X
APP Y

PREFACE

The results of several years of conferences, research, teaching, revisions and try-outs have gone into the making of this manual. Much of the initial work was made possible by the support of the Merrill-Palmer Institute.

The objective was to construct a manual that presented a balanced and realistic approach. If a "trade-off" had to be made between including material based on research, experience, and theory, the decision was almost invariably in favor of research and experience.

In its present form the manual has been used as an effective teaching-aid by a large number of people with various backgrounds and with various levels of skill, experience, and interest in reading instruction. The present version has been used most frequently in helping children learn to read. But it can and has been used, with appropriate changes in phrasing, as a guide in teaching illiterate adults to read.

While it is impossible to acknowledge individually all of the people who have contributed in some way to the work on which the manual is based, the following people deserve special mention. Solomon Schimmel and Kathy Frerichs worked hard and with dedication on early versions of the manual. My wife Donna provided a great deal of technical assistance with enduring patience and good cheer. And Anona Ferguson served as the secretary-typist who managed to make things easier for everyone.

CONTENTS

INTRODUCTION   xi

INDEXES:

    Letter and Sound Relations   xxvii

    Selected Reading Rules   xxxix

    Supplementary Spelling Rules   xli

    Selected Word Lists   xliii

SECTIONS:

    I.   Single Letter—Single Consonant Sound   1

    II.   Single Letter—Single Short Vowel Sound   3

    III.   Single Letter—Two Consonant Sounds   7

    IV. Two Letter Spelling—Single Consonant Sound   9

    V.   Two Letter Spelling—Two Consonant Sounds   13

    VI. Some Consonant Letter-Sound Combinations with Single Short
          Vowel Sounds   19

    VII. Single Letter—Two or More Short Vowel Sounds   27

    VIII. Two Letter Spelling—One or More Vowel Sounds   31

    IX. Single Letter and "Silent" *e*—Single Long Vowel Sound   35

    X.   General Rule for Single Vowel Letter—Short or Long Sound   41

    XI. Single Letter *y*—Vowel Sounds   45

XII.	Two Letter Spelling—Single Long Vowel Sound	**49**
XIII.	Two Letter Spelling—Two Vowel Sounds	**51**
XIV.	Two Letter Spelling—Vowel-Consonant Combination Sounds Involving *l* and *r*	**57**
XV.	Three Letter Spelling—Vowel-Consonant Combination Sounds Involving *r*	**67**
XVI.	Some Words Pronounced or Spelled the Same Way	**69**
XVII.	Review of Sounds for Two Letter Spellings *ch, ph, gh, qu*	**73**
XVIII.	Some *Regular* Letter-Sound Combinations at *Beginning* and *End* of Words	**77**
XIX.	Some *Irregular* Letter-Sound Combinations at *End* of Words	**89**
XX.	Silent Consonant Letters	**107**
XXI.	Some Common Words and Some Irregular Words	**111**

APPENDIX X   115

APPENDIX Y   121

REFERENCES   125

INTRODUCTION

This manual is for teachers, parents, teacher aides, and volunteer tutors who are trying to help children read. As a guide, it should be especially useful to those teachers, parents, teacher aides, and volunteer tutors who have had little or no previous formal preparation in teaching reading.

It is organized in terms of the sound and letter relations involved in reading. These relations are presented in a step-by-step fashion with accompanying illustrations, lists of words, rule statements, and suggestions. Since essentially *all* of the sound and letter relations required to read American English are covered in the manual, it can be used as a guide in helping any student to read, regardless of his grade placement or age.

If you are a regular classroom teacher you may want to use the manual as a supplement to a reading series or to a language program which you already have in operation in your classroom. On the other hand, you may want to use it as the basis of a step-by-step program in reading instruction. It can and has been used both ways. The sound and letter relations discussed in the manual are consistent, for the most part, with those presented in various reading series or language programs, so it is a simple matter to coordinate the two. If the manual is used more as the basis for a general program, however, there is the added advantage of being able to select stories and exercises for reading from among the wide range of materials currently available on the open commercial market. In either event, teachers who have used the manual report that they particularly like it because it is a handy desk reference on sound and letter relations, and because its word lists are conveniently used for a variety of classroom reading and spelling activities.

If you are a parent, and are trying to help a single child or a small group of children to read, you will probably feel compelled to rely heavily on a guide like this one. If you don't become compulsive or literal about everything you'll be all right. A good approach is to keep things zipping along and much like a game. If you systematically devote about 10–15 minutes once a day to dealing with a given sound and letter relation, and then devote another 5 minutes to reviewing it or some other relation at another point during the day, that should be more than enough time. Assuming you are doing things right, you should be able to record some marked improvement in a child's reading skill within a few days. Your best bet, of course, is to coordinate what you do with what the child's teacher does. If you both have a copy of this manual, it will be much easier for you to follow through in a supplemental way on whatever the child's teacher suggests.

If you are a teacher aid or volunteer tutor, you also will probably feel compelled to rely heavily on a guide like this one. If you don't become compulsive or literal about everything you'll be all right too. As in the case of a parent, try to give your teaching activities some zip. Systematically deal with one relation every day, and then review it or another one once every day. If you're doing things right, it should be possible for you to record within a few days some marked improvement in a child's reading skill. Whether you're helping a small group of children or one child to read, your best bet also is, of course, to take your cues from the child's or children's regular classroom teacher. If you both have a copy of this manual, and have studied it enough so that you both have a pretty good understanding of what's covered, you'll find it's an easy matter to coordinate the "what" and "how" of your teaching activities and their effectiveness.

In keeping with the idea that the manual should be as convenient and efficient to use as possible, it is worth noting here that a number of indexes have been included at the very beginning of the manual. One shows you on what page and in what section a given letter-sound or letter-sound combination is discussed. One shows you on what page and in what section a given reading rule is presented. Another one shows you on what page and in what section certain lists of words are presented. And, although the emphasis is on reading not spelling in this manual, one index shows you on what page and in what section supplementary spelling rules are presented.

There are also two things you will meet in the text of the manual that are worth mentioning here. First, *when you see parentheses around a word in a list it usually indicates that the word can be pronounced in another way, or it is spelled differently, or it is a further illustration.* Second, when you see the phrase "If no sense . . . ," it usually means the word doesn't sound right using a previous sound(s) or that the word doesn't make sense in the context of what's being read. By "sound right" we mean that the word does not sound like a word the child knows and/or like a word at all.

As you make use of the manual you probably will discover a number of things about reading that have escaped your attention in the past. Perhaps the chief thing to alert you to at this point, however, is the order that exists in the sound-letter relations of our spoken-written language, and upon which the manual has been based. There are undoubtedly many ways to illustrate this. But one of the best ways I can think of to show you this is to give you a summary overview of sound-letter relations. As it turns out, if you're like most people, a summary overview may be of help to you in two other ways. It may help you to see some other things that are worth knowing about reading. And it may enable you to make better and wider use of the manual.

Let's begin by taking a didactic look at the sound-letter relations in American English. Most of the sound-letter correspondences in American English can be summarized as in Table 1. Now, don't let the size of the table scare you. It's really a very straightforward table.

The furthermost column to the left shows the sound symbols used in the pronunciation key by Thorndike and Barnhart (T-B) in their High School Dictionary (1965). This key is representative of dictionary keys in general, and we are using it simply because it is convenient.

The next column shows the phoneme symbols which correspond to the T-B symbols. The More Frequent and Less Frequent spelling columns show some of the more and some of the less frequent ways each sound is spelled. The designations "More" and "Less" are somewhat arbitrary in places. But, in the main, they do reflect the way a sound is likely to be spelled.

For the most part, Table 1 is an adaptation of one by Hall (1961) using the phoneme notation system of Trager and Smith (1951). Hall's table, in turn, is an adaptation of an earlier one by Soffietti (1955). Hall and Soffietti are both linguists. Interestingly enough, however, Soffietti is among those who have stressed the inconsistency of sound-letter corre-spondences, while Hall is among those who have stressed the consistency. We'll come back to this point in a moment.

First, let me point out that both the Thorndike and Barnhart pronuncia-tion key and Hall's phoneme list make some distinctions in sounds that are not retained in Table 1. The Thorndike and Barnhart key, for example, makes a distinction between the sounds ã as in "prayer" and e as in "bread." Things are simplified by treating these two as one sound; the short vowel sound e. The same thing holds for the Thorndike and Barnhart distinction among the sounds o, ô, and ä. All three are essentially the same short vowel sound o. The so-called all-purpose muttering vowel ə is also used by Thorndike and Barnhart since it does not have a sound *exactly* like that of any of the short vowel sounds. It is very much like the short vowel sound u, however, and it is treated that way in Table 1.

Hall also makes several notational distinctions in phonemes that are not retained in Table 1. He includes in his table, for example, the phonemes /way/ as in the oi of cho*i*r, /wə/ as in the o..e of *one*, and /ŋ/ as in the ng of si*ng*. To the everyday listener or speaker these sounds are adequately

Table 1. Sound and Letter Relations

Sound		More Frequent Spelling		Less Frequent Spelling	
T-B Symbol	Phoneme	Letter	Word Example	Letter	Word Example
a	/æ/	a	bat	ai	plaid
				ay	prayer
				au	laugh
e, (ã)	/e/	e	bet	ae	aesthetic
		ea	feather	ei	their
				ie	friend
				eo	leopard
				oe	foetid
				ai	said
				a	any
				u	bury
				ay	says
i	/i/	i	fit	ie	sieve
		ui	build	e	engineer
		y	myth	ee	been
				o	women
				u	busy
o, (ô, ä)	/o/, /a/	o	odd	ou	bought
		a	watch	oa	broad
		al	walk	ah	Utah
		au	taught	e	sergeant
		aw	law	ea	heart
u, (ə)	/ə/	u	sun	ai	fountain
		a	about	ia	parliament
		ou	couple	e	moment
		o	son	i	easily
				eo	dungeon
				oo	flood
				oe	does
				ei	villein
				oi	porpoise
ā	/ey/	a . . . e	rate	ei	veil
		ai	rain	ea	steak
		ay	say	ey	obey
				au	gauge

		More Frequent Spelling		Less Frequent Spelling	
Sound					
T-B Symbol	Phoneme	Letter	Word Example	Letter	Word Example
ē	/iy/	e . . . e	theme	i	machine
		e	equal	ae	caesarian
		ee	keep	eo	people
		ea	tea	oe	phoenix
		ei	receive	ay	quay
		ie	thief		
		y	happy		
		ey	key		
ī	/ay/	i . . . e	ice	ei	height
		i	iodine	uy	buy
		ie	tie	ay	aye
		y	sky	ai	aisle
		ye	lye		
ō	/ow/	o . . . e	note	ou	soul
		o	odor	eau	beau
		oa	boat	eo	yeoman
		oe	toe	ew	sew
		ow	blow	oo	brooch
ū	/yuw/	u . . . e	use	ue	cue
		u	union	ew	few
				eu	feud
				eau	beauty
				ieu	adieu
				iew	view
				yu . . e	yule
				you	you
u̇	/u/	oo	book	u	put
				o	wolf
				ou	should
ü	/uw/	oo	moon	ou	group
		u . . . e	tune	ui	fruit
		ue	blue	oe	shoe
		ew	drew	o . . . e	prove
				wo	two
				eu	maneuver

Table 1 (Continued)

Sound		More Frequent Spelling		Less Frequent Spelling	
T-B Symbol	Phoneme	Letter	Word Example	Letter	Word Example
ou	/aw/	ow	how		
		ou	out		
oi	/oi/	oi	soil		
		oy	boy		
ėr, (ər)	/ər/	ur	burn	ear	heard
		er	term	yr	zephyr
		ir	first		
		or	word		
		ar	liar		
		our	journey		
b	/b/	b	bit		
		bb	cobbler		
d	/d/	d	dip		
		dd	saddle		
		ed	spilled		
f	/f/	f	fine	gh	tough
		ff	puff		
		ph	phrase		
g	/g/	g	get	gh	ghost
		gg	gaggle	gu	guest
h	/h/	h	hot	wh	whose
j	/ǧ/	j	joint	d	graduate
		g	tragic	di	soldier
		dg	fudge	du	verdure
k	/k/	k	keep	cu	biscuit
		c	catch	cq	acquire
		ck	black	cch	bacchanal
		cc	account	cque	sacque
		ch	character	qu	liquor
				q	barbeque

T-B Symbol	Phoneme	More Frequent Spelling		Less Frequent Spelling	
		Letter	Word Example	Letter	Word Example
l	/l/	l	like		
		ll	toll		
m	/m/	m	milk		
		mm	hammer		
n	/n/	n	nice		
		nn	banner		
p	/p/	p	pint		
		pp	slipper		
kw	/kw/	qu	quite		
r	/r/	r	rank	rh	rhythm
		rr	parrot		
s	/s/	s	seat	sch	schism
		ss	boss		
		c	cent		
		sc	scene		
sh	/š/	sh	shop	ch	machine
		ci	special	sci	conscience
		si	mansion	sch	schist
		ti	nation	ce	ocean
				s	sure
				se	nauseous
				ss	tissue
ch	/č/	ch	chance	t	natural
		tch	patch	te	righteous
		tu	future	ti	question
hw	/hw/	wh	which		
th	/θ/	th	thick		
Th	/ð/	th	then		
t	/t/	t	top	th	thyme
		tt	tattle		
		ed	stopped		

Table 1 (Continued)

Sound		More Frequent Spelling		Less Frequent Spelling	
T-B Symbol	Phoneme	Letter	Word Example	Letter	Word Example
v	/v/	v	vest	f	of
		vv	savvy	ph	Stephen
w	/w/	w	went	u	quiet
ks	/ks/	x	fix		
y	/y/	y	yank	i	onion
				j	hallelujah
z	/z/	z	zombie	ss	scissors
		zz	drizzle	sc	discern
		s	has	x	xenophon
zh	/ž/	s	treasure	z	azure
		si	division	zi	brazier
				g	garage

indicated by other sounds. In addition, no distinction is made in Table 1 between the phonemes /o/ and /a/. For our purposes, the phoneme /a/ has essentially the same sound as /o/—the short vowel sound o.

At first glance it looks like Soffietti and the others who have stressed the inconsistency of sound-letter correspondences are right. A count shows that there are some 44 sound symbols and some 42 phoneme symbols in Table 1. However, a count of both the More and Less Frequent spellings shows that there are some 227 different spellings for these sounds or phonemes. This means that on the average there are about five spellings for each sound. On the other hand, there is a range of from 2 to 13 different ways to spell a particular sound. And, by looking over Table 1, you also can see that in general there are more ways to spell a given vowel sound than there are to spell a given consonant sound.

Now, in terms of what children must learn in order to become pretty good readers, are things really as bad as all of this suggests? No. Things aren't this bad. The cards have been stacked.

As it turns out, all that has been shown so far is that if you start with the assumption that sound-letter correspondences are terribly inconsistent, you can build a seemingly convincing case that they are. By considering in a detailed way all possible spellings of a sound, regardless of how rare or trivial, you merely highlight the variability of sound-letter relations and thereby play down any consistencies.

You can see what I'm getting at if you'll look at Table 1 again, only this time ignore the less frequent spellings. As we will see later on, some of these spellings are regular enough in some way to warrant teaching and learning them. Others however are simply exceptions or rarities in the way a sound is spelled. And they occur so seldom that when they are involved in a common word which a child must know for his reading, they are most readily learned at first as sight words. A large amount of the seeming variability in sound-letter correspondences in Table 1 can be eliminated by recognizing the limited importance of many of the less frequent spellings.

The inclusion of the double-letter spellings of consonant sounds in Table 1 also is designed to make things look worse than they really are. It is actually a simple matter to learn that in reading one makes one sound for these.

Their inclusion in Table 1 does bring up, however, a matter that is important and related. It has been estimated that while 1 or 2 out of every 10 American children have some difficulty in reading, 1 out of every 3 has difficulty in spelling. Does that surprise you? I remember the first time I read a statement like this somewhere, and it sure surprised me. But maybe it shouldn't be surprising. After all, there are fewer sounds for a given letter or letter combination than there are ways to spell a given sound.

What that means is that you have more choices from among which to choose in spelling than you do in reading a word. I can show you this very simply. We merely take what is presented in Table 1 and rearrange it as in Table 2. This new table now shows us most of the different sounds for a particular letter or letter combination in American English. At this point the consonant double letters and so-called silent letters are of no consequence to us, so they are omitted from the table. Also, in making up this table for you, I have tried—where possible—to list the sounds for a particular letter or letter combination according to their roughly judged order of importance for someone trying to read American English.

The sound symbols used in this table are the same as those of Thorndike and Barnhart, with a few exceptions. In place of Thorndike and Barnhart's symbols u̇, ü, and ou for, respectively, the short and long sounds of *oo* and sound of *ow*, we have used the symbols oo, o͞o, and ow. And, in place of their sound and symbol ėr (and ər), we have used the sound and symbol ur.

If you study this table a bit, you will see that even though we have included rarely made sounds for particular letters, there are no more than six different sounds for any letter or letter combination. In fact, for most of the vowel single letter and letter combinations there are only two or three vowel sounds that are frequently made.

Table 2. *Different Sounds of Letters*

Letter	Sounds	Word Example	Letter	Sounds	Word Example
a	a	at		i	sieve
	o	watch	ey	ē	key
	u	about		ā	obey
	ā	ate	eo	u	dungeon
	e	any		ē	people
ae	e	aerial		e	leopard
	ē	aeon		ō	yeoman
a(h)	o	Utah	eu	ōō	maneuver
a(l)	o	walk		ū	feud
	a	scalp	ew	ōō	drew
aw	o	draw		ū	few
au	o	taught		ō	sew
	ā	gauge	i	i	fit
	a	laugh		ī	bite
ai	ā	rain		u	flirt, easily
	u	fountain		ē	machine
	e	said	ia	u	parliament
	a	plaid	o	o	hot
	ī	aisle		ō	open
ay	ā	say		u	son, worm
	e	says		ōō	move, to
	ī	aye		oo	wolf
	a	prayer		i	women
	ē	quay	oa	ō	boat
e	e	bet		o	broad
	ē	equal	oo	ōō	food
	u	moment		oo	book
	i	engineer		u	flood
	o	sergeant		ō	brooch
ea	ē	tea	oe	ō	toe
	e	feather		ōō	shoe
	u	heard		u	does
	ā	steak		ē	phoenix
	o	heart	ow	ow	how
ee	ē	seem		ō	blow
	i	been	ou	ow	trout
ei	ē	receive		u	couple, journey
	ā	weight		ōō	group
	e	their		ō	soul
	ī	height		o	ought
	u	villein		oo	should
ie	ē	thief	oi	oi	boil
	ī	tie		u	porpoise
	e	friend	oy	oi	toy

Letter	Sounds	Word Example	Letter	Sounds	Word Example
u	u	cup, burn	k	k	keep
	ū	union	l	l	let
	o͞o	rule	m	m	milk
	oo	put	n	n	nice
	e	bury	p	p	pint
	i	busy	ph	f	trophy
ue	o͞o	blue		v	Stephen
	ū	cue	qu	kw	quite
ui	i	build	r	r	run
	o͞o	fruit	s	s	seat
uy	ī	buy		z	has
wo	o͞o	two	s(e), ss	s	base, grass
y	y	yank		sh	nauseous, tissue
	ē	happy	s(i)	s	basic
	ī	sky		sh	mansion
	i	myth		zh	division
	u	zephyr	s(u)	s	sulk
ye	i	rye		zh	measure
b	b	bit	sc	sk	scat
c	s	cent		s	scene
	k	cramp		z	discern
cc	k	account	sh	sh	shop
	ks	accent	t	t	top
ch	ch	chance	t(c)	t	ate
	k	character		ch	righteous
	sh	machine	t(u)	ch	future
d	d	did		t	attitude
ed	ed	red	t(i)	t	gratify
	d	spilled		sh	notion
	t	talked		ch	question
f	f	fine	th	th	thick
	v	of		Th	then
gh	silent	thought		t	thyme
	g	ghost	v	v	very
	f	tough	w	w	went
g	g	get	wh	hw	which
	j	magic		h	who
	zh	garage	x	ks	box
h	h	hot		z	Xenophon
j	j	just	z	z	zero
	y	hallelujah		zh	azure

We can begin to see then why fewer children may have problems in reading than in spelling. There are fewer possible sounds which have to be learned for particular spellings than there are possible spellings which have to be learned for particular sounds. This also may help to explain why most children find it easier to become a pretty good reader than to become a pretty good speller.

That's all there is to say about what Table 2 shows us at this point. So let's go back to Table 1 for a moment—and the way it stacks the cards. There are two more things to mention. First, if you continued to analyze and rearrange Table 1 in various ways you would discover eventually, as others have, that it obscures many regularities in sound-letter relations. Second, greater simplification is possible in what is required in learning to read than the table even begins to suggest.

But you don't have to take just my word for it. To enable you to see that this is so, Tables 3-A and 3-B have been constructed. Taken together the two tables represent a first approximation, at least, of what is perhaps an optimum degree of simplification. Each has been organized to show what sound or sounds must occur for particular spellings. When a child already can utter the sound or sounds indicated he, of course, does not have to learn these. All that has to happen is that the particular spellings shown come to control these already established sounds.

You should also note that, unlike the case in Table 1, not all of the sounds listed in Tables 3–A and 3–B consist of a single isolated sound or phoneme. A given tabled sound, as a unit, may be made up of several sounds. It is still a single sound, however, in relation to its spelling.

In one way or another, Tables 3–A and 3–B include practically everything presented in Table 1. Even almost all of the exceptions and irregularities indicated in the Less Frequent spelling column of Table 1 have been incorporated in some reasonable way in these tables. We should also note that the entries in Table 3–B with a single bracket around them involve sound-letter correspondences that already are covered in some way in Table 3–A, while those with a double bracket around them supplement other entries in Table 3–B. In both cases, they are included as separate entries only because of their judged importance on other grounds.

Now, you'll recall that we said there are some 227 different spellings of some 40+ sounds shown in Table 1. What does a count of the entries in Tables 3–A and 3–B combined reveal? Well, you may be surprised by the results. Here they are.

A simple count—not including the silent letters—gives a total of 125 sound-letter entries. There are 140 spellings, as compared to the 227 in Table 1. (If we don't count the bracketed entries these figures become even more impressive—98 sound-letter entries and 113 spellings.)

There is, however, even more order than these figures suggest in what has to be learned to read effectively. Of the 125 sound-letter entries in the

Table 3–A. One-Letter and Two-Letter Spellings and Sounds

Spelling	Number of Sounds			
	One Sound	Two Sounds	Three Sounds	Four or Five Sounds
	Letter(s)—Sound	Letter(s)—Sound	Letter(s)—Sound	Letter(s)—Sound
Single Letter	a . . e—**ā** e . . e—**ē** i . . e—**ī** o . . e—**ō** b—**b** d—**d** f—**f** h—**h** j—**j** k—**k** l—**l** m—**m** n—**n** p—**p** r—**r** s—**s** t—**t** v—**v** w—**w** x—**ks** z—**z**	e—**e, ē** i—**i, ī** u—**u, ū** u . . e—**o͞o, ū** c—**k, s** g—**g, j**	o—**o, ō, u**	a—**a, u, o, ā** y—**y, ē, ī, i**
Two Letters	ee—**ē** ck—**k** ph—**f** qu—**kw** sh—**sh**	ie—**ē, ī** ow—**ow, ō** oo—**o͞o, oo** ui—**i, o͞o** ed—**d, t** cc—**k, ks** sc—**sk, s** th—**th, Th** wh—**hw, h** or—**ōr, ur** er—**ur, er** ir—**ur, ir** ur—**ur, ūr**	ea—**ē, e, (ā)** ch—**ch, k, sh** gh—**none, g, f**	ou—**ow, u, o͞o, ō, (o)** ar—**or, ur, er, ōr**
Multiple Two Letters	ai, ay—**ā** oa, oe—**ō** oi, oy—**oi** aw, au—**o**	ei, ey—**ē, ā** ew, ue—**o͞o, ū**		

Table 3–B. Letter Combinations and Sounds; and Silent Letters

Spelling	Number of Sounds			Silent Letters
	One Sound	Two Sounds	Three Sounds	
	Letters—Sound	Letters—Sound	Letters-Sound	Letters
Letter Combination	ible—**ubl**	able—**ābl, ubl**	ear—**ēr, er, ur**	b
	sure—**zhur**	ance—**ans, uns**	our—**ur, owr, ōr**	d
	ial—**ēul**	tain—**tān, tun**	age—**āj, ij, oj**	g
	ous—**us**	sion—**shun, zhun**	ine—**īn, in, ēn**	h
	ious—**ēus**	tion—**shun, chun**		k
	ence—**uns**	ior—**yur, ēur**	⌈ de—**dē, di, de** ⌉	l
	dence—**duns**	eon—**ēon, un**	re—**rē, ri, re**	t
	sive—**siv**	ace—**ās, is**	pre—**prē, pri,**	w
	tive—**tiv**	ate—**āt, it**	**pre**	p
	eau—**ō**	ice—**īs, is**	pro—**pro, prō,**	n
	igh—**ī**	ile—**īl, il**	⌊ **pru** ⌋	⌈ gh ⌉
	ough—**ō**	ite—**īt, it**	⌈ ti—**ti, sh, ch** ⌉	
	eigh—**ā**	ive—**īv, iv**	tu—**tōo, chōo,**	
	gue—**g**		**chu**	
	que—**k**	⌈ co—**ko, kō** ⌉	ia—**ēu, u, yu**	
		com—**kom, kum**	⌊ io—**ēu, ēō, u** ⌋	
	⌈ ment—**ment**	con—**kon, kun**		
	ness—**nes**	di—**di, dī**		
	dis—**dis**	par—**por, per**		
	en—**en**	per—**pur, per**		
	ex—**eks**	⌊ pos—**pōs, pos** ⌋		
	im—**im**	⟦ ie—**ēu, u** ⟧		
	in—**in**			
	un—**un**			
	sub—**sub**			
	⌊ trans—**trans**			
	⟦ iu—**ēu**			
Letter Combinations	ture, tur—**chur**		ion, ian—**un, yun, ēun**	
	cial, tial—**shul**			
	cious, tious—**shus**			
	ought, aught—**ot**			
	al, el, il, ol, ul, le —**ul**			

two tables combined, 61 are in the One Sound columns. In 52 of these 61 instances only one spelling and one sound are involved. And, in all but one of the remaining 9 instances, only two spellings and one sound are involved.

Making a count of the entries in the other columns of the two tables, we also find that there are 41 entries which involve learning two sounds for one spelling, 16 which involve learning three sounds for one spelling, 3 which involve learning four sounds for one spelling, and 1 which involves learning five sounds for one spelling. Of the 3 remaining instances, 2 involve learning two sounds for each of two spellings and 1 involves learning three sounds for each of two spellings.

On the basis of these counts, it is clear that there is more simplicity and order in what has to be learned to read effectively than Table 1 suggests and many people have claimed. There are a limited number of sound-letter correspondences to learn. And the majority of them involve only one or two sounds for one spelling.

But what about the case where there are, for example, four possible sounds for a particular spellling? In this case, must learning which sound to say end up being a matter of confusion? The answer is that it often has ended up that way, but it doesn't have to. We can always take some additional step that will simplify things. We can, for example, always teach a rule or cue that determines which sound to utter in a specific instance. The rule may be no more than an arbitrary one of, "Try this sound, and then this one."—for a two sound spelling. Or the cue may be no more than, "When this spelling is here in a word, we say this sound; when it's here, we say this one." Fortunately, regardless of how crude they may be, rules and cues can help to make even the seemingly difficult task of learning which of four sounds to say a relatively easy one.

Let's end this overview of sound-letter relations by summarizing what we have covered. We started off by pointing out that in American English there are about forty sounds and a large number of ways of spelling them. We agreed that there is a fair amount of inconsistency in sound-letter correspondences. We then proceeded to argue, however, that there is more consistency in sound-letter relations than at first meets the eye. We tried to show two things by various tables and counts. First, order or regularity can be found in many so-called inconsistent sound-letter relations. Second, it is possible to bring about much simplification and order in what a person has to learn in order to read.

There remains only a final word or two to be said about the manual and about your flexible use of it. As you will see, there is a progression to the 21 sections. But if you deviate from it, there is no reason to feel you are committing a sin. Also, as pointed out earlier, the material included should prove to be comprehensive and complete. But you may never have occasion where you need or want to make use of everything presented. The key thing to remember is that the manual was designed to be a guide, not a prescription. Also, as a handy desk reference, it can be consulted and used much like a dictionary.

INDEX

Letter and Sound Relations

Letter	Sound	Page	Section
a	ă	3 6; 27; 28 29	II-A, B; VII-A-1; VII-A-3
	u	27; 28-29; 97, 98	VII-A-1; VII-A-3; XIX-C-1a
	o	27-29	VII-A-2, 3
	ā	41	X-A
a . . e	ā	35-39	IX-A, B, C
able	ābl	94	XIX-B-1a
	ubl	94	XIX-B-lb
ace	ās	100	XIX-D-3a
	is	100-101	XIX-D-3b
	(us)	100-101	XIX-D-3b
age	āj	100	XIX-D-3a
	ij	100-101	XIX-D-3b
	(uj)	100-101	XIX-D-3b
	oj	101	XIX-D-3b(1)
ai	ā	49	XII-A
air	er	67	XV-A-1
al (l)	ol	27-28	VII-A-2
	al	28	VII-A-2a
	ul	57	XIV-A
ance	ans	94-95	XIX-B-2a
	uns	94-95	XIX-B-2b

Letter	Sound	Page	Section
ar	or	27-28; 62-63	VII-A-2; XIV-C-1
	ur	63	XIV-C-1a
	er	64; 67-68	XIV-C-1a(2); XV-A-2
	u, r	65	XIV-C-1c
ard	urd	63	XIV-C-1a(1)
	(ord)	63	XIV-C-1a(1)
are	er	67	XV-A-1
arr	er	64; 67-68	XIV-C-1a(2); XV-A-2
	ur	65	XIV-C-1c
arry	erē	64; 67-68	XIV-C-1a(2); XV-A-2
	urē	64	XIV-C-1a(2)(a)
ate	āt	100	XIX-D-3a
	it	100-101	XIX-D-3b
	(ut)	100-101	XIX-D-3b
au	o	31	VIII-A
aught	ot	93	XIX-A-17
aw	o	31	VIII-A
ay	ā	49	XII-A

---

b	b	1-2	I-B
	silent	109	XX-B-1
bb	b	9-10	IV-A-2

---

c	k	7; 16	III-A-1; V-G-1
	s	7; 16	III-A-2; V-G-2
cc	k	15-16	V-F-1; V-G-1
	ks	16	V-F-2; V-G-2
ch	ch	13; 73	V-B-1; XVII-A-1
	k	14; 73	V-B-2; XVII-A-2
	(sh)	74	XVII-A-2a
ci	sh	97-98; 105	XIX-C-1a; XIX-D-7b
cial	shul	90	XIX-A-5

Letter	Sound	Page	Section
cious	shus	91	XIX-A-9
ck	k	11 ; 16	IV-B-2 ; V-G-1
co	ko	80	XVIII-C-1a
	kō	80	XVIII-C-1b
com	kom	81	XVIII-C-2a
	kum	81	XVIII-C-2b
	(ku, m)	81	XVIII-C-2b(1)
con	kon	81-82	XVIII-C-3a, c
	kun	82	XVIII-C-3b, c
d	d	1-2	I-B
	cilont	107	XX-A-1
de	dē	85	XVIII-D-1a
	di	85	XVIII-D-1a
	de	85	XVIII-D-1b
dence	duns	92	XIX-A-11
dd	d	9-10	IV-A-2
dge	j	107	XX-A-1
di	di	82	XVIII-C-4a
	dī	83	XVIII-C-4b
dis	dis	78	XVIII-B-1
e	e	3-5	II-A, B
	ē	41-42	X-A, B
e . . e	ē	35-39	IX-A, B, C-1, 2, 4
ea	ē	53-54	XIII-C-1
	e	54	XIII-C-2
	(ā)	54	XIII-C-2
ear	ēr	68	XV-B-1
	er	68	XV-B-2
	ur	68	XV-B-3

Letter	Sound	Page	Section
eau	ō	92	XIX-A-14
ed	d	17	V-H-1
	t	17	V-H-2
	ud	17	V-H-1a
ee	ē	50	XII-B
ei	ē	55	XIII-D-1
	ā	55	XIII-D-2
eigh	ā	94	XIX-A-18
eight	āt	94	XIX-A-18
el	ul	57	XIV-A
en	en	78	XVIII-B-2
ence	uns	91-92	XIX-A-10
eon	ēon	99	XIX-D-1a
	un	99	XIX-D-1b
er	ur	39; 57-58	IX-C-4; XIV-B-1
	er	58-59, 60; 68	XIV-B-1a, 4; XV-A-3
err	er	68	XV-A-3
et	ā	109	XX-A-6
ew	o͞o	32	VIII-C
	ū	32	VIII-C-1
ex	eks	78	XVIII-B-3
ey	ē	55	XIII-D-1
	ā	55	XIII-D-2
f	f	1	I-A
ff	f	9-10	IV-A-1, 2
fy	fī	46	XI-B-1a
g	g	8	III-B-1
	j	8	III-B-2, 3
	silent	108	XX-A-3

Letter	Sound	Page	Section
gg	**g**	10	IV-A-2
gh	**silent**	15 ; 74 ; 93-94 ; 108	V-D-1 ; XVII-C-1 ; XIX-A-15, 16, 17, 18 ; XX-A-4
	g	15 ; 75	V-D-2 ; XVII-C-2
	f	75 ; 93	XVII-C-3 ; XIX-A-16
gi	**j**	97-98 ; 105	XIX-C-1a ; XIX-D-7b
gn	**n**	108	XX-A-3
gue	**g**	100	XIX-D-2c

h	**h**	2	I-C
	silent	109	XX-B-2

i	**i**	3-5	II-A, B
	ī	41	X-A
i . . e	**ī**	35-39	IX-A, B, C
ia	**ēu**	104	XIX-D-7a
	u	105	XIX-D-7b
	yu	105	XIX-D-7b(1)
	(ēyu)	105	XIX-D-7b(1)
ial	**ēul**	90 ; 104	XIX-A-4 ; XIX-D-7a
ible	**ubl**	89	XIX-A-1
ice	**īs**	101	XIX-D-4a
	is	101-102	XIX-D-4b
ie	**ēu**	104	XIX-D-7a
	u	105	XIX-D-7b
igh	**ī**	93	XIX-A-15
ight	**īt**	93	XIX-A-15
il	**ul**	57	XIV-A
ile	**īl**	101	XIX-D-4a
	il	101-102	XIX-D-4b

Letter	Sound	Page	Section
im	**im**	78-79	XVIII-B-4
in	**in**	79	XVIII-B-5
ind	**īnd**	43	X-E
	ind	43	X-E-1
ine	**īn**	101	XIX-D-4a
	in	101-102	XIX-D-4b
	ēn	102	XIX-D-4b(1)
ing	**ing**	24 ; 38	VI-C-1 ; IX-C-1
io	**ēu**	104-105	XIX-D-7a
	u	105	XIX-D-7b
	ēō	105	XIX-D-7a(1)
ion	**un**	97-98	XIX-C-1a
	yun	98	XIX-C-1b
	ēun	98	XIX-C-1c
	(ēyun)	98	XIX-C-1c
ior	**yur**	97	XIX-B-6a
	ēur	97 ; 104	XIX-B-6b ; XIX-D-7a
	(ēyur)	97	XIX-B-6b
ious	**ēus**	91	XIX-A-8
ir	**ur**	59, 60	XIV-B-2, 4
	ir	59, 60	XIV-B-2a, 4
ite	**īt**	101	XIX-D-4a
	it	101-102	XIX-D-4b
iu	**ēu**	104-105	XIX-D-7a
ive	**īv**	101	XIX-D-4a
	iv	101-102	XIX-D-4b
j	**j**	1-2	I-B
k	**k**	1-2	I-B
	silent	107-108	XX-A-2
kn	**n**	107-108	XX-A-2

Letter	Sound	Page	Section
l	**l**	1	I-A
	silent	110	XX-B-3
le	**ul**	39 ; 57	IX-C-5 ; XIV-A
ll	**l**	9-10	IV-A-1, 2

Letter	Sound	Page	Section
m	**m**	1	I-A
ment	**ment**	77	XVIII-A-1
mm	**m**	10	IV-A-2
mn	**n**	109	XX-A-7

Letter	Sound	Page	Section
n	**n**	1	I-A
	silent	109	XX-A-7
ness	**nes**	77	XVIII-A-2
nn	**n**	10	IV-A-2

Letter	Sound	Page	Section
o	**o**	3-5 ; 29	II-A, B ; VII-B-1, 2
	u	29	VII-B-1, 2
	ō	41, 42	X-A, C
o . . e	**ō**	35-39	IX-A, B, C-1, 2, 3, 4
oa	**ō**	50	XII-C
oe	**ō**	50	XII-C
oi	**oi**	32-33	VIII-D
ol	**ul**	57	XIV-A
old	**ōld**	42	X-D
oll	**ōl**	42	X-D
	ol	42	X-D-1
olt	**ōlt**	42	X-D

Letter	Sound	Page	Section
on	**un**	29 ; 97-98	VII-B-1 ; XIX-C-1a
oo	**ōo**	32	VIII-B-1
	oo	32	VIII-B-2
or	**ōr**	60-61	XIV-B-5
	ur	29 ; 61-62	VII-B-1 ; XIV-B-5a
ost	**ōst**	42	X-D
	ost	42	X-D-1
oth	**uth**	29	VII-B-1
ou	**ow**	33	VIII-E-1
	u	33 ; 93	VIII-E-2 ; XIX-A-16
	ōo	33-34	VIII-E-3
	ō	33-34	VIII-E-3
	o	34 ; 93	VIII-E-4 ; XIX-A-16, 17
ough	**ō**	93	XIX-A-16
ought	**ot**	93	XIX-A-17
our	**ur**	65	XIV-C-2a
	owr	65-66	XIV-C-2b(1)
	ōr	65-66	XIV-C-2b(2)
ous	**us**	91	XIX-A-7
ow	**ow**	51	XIII-A-1
	ō	51-52	XIII-A-2
oy	**oi**	32-33	VIII-D

---

p	**p**	1-2	I-B
	silent	110	XX-B-4
par	**por**	83	XVIII-C-5a
	per	83	XVIII-C-5b
per	**pur**	84	XVIII-C-6a
	per	84	XVIII-C-6b
ph	**f**	11 ; 74	IV-B-4 ; XVII-B-1
pos	**pōs**	84	XVIII-C-7a
	pos	84	XVIII-C-7b

xxxiv INDEX

Letter	Sound	Page	Section
pp	**p**	10	IV-A-2
pre	**prē**	87	XVIII-D-3a, b
	prī	87	XVIII-D-3b
	pre	87	XVIII-D-3c
pro	**pro**	87-88	XVIII-D-4a
	prō	88	XVIII-D-4b, c
	pru	88	XVIII-D-4c
qu	**kw**	11 ; 75-76	IV-B-3 ; XVII-D-1
qua	**kwo**	27-28 ; 75-76	VII-A-2 ; XVII-D-1
quar	**kwor**	65	XIV-C-1b
que	**k**	100	XIX-D-2c
r	**r**	1	I-A
re	**rē**	85-86	XVIII-D-2a, b
	ri	86	XVIII-D-2b
	re	86	XVIII-D-2c
rr	**r**	10	IV-A-2
s	**s**	1	I-A
sc	**sk**	15 ; 16-17	V-E-1 ; V-G-3
	s	15 ; 16-17	V-E-2 ; V-G-3
sh	**sh**	11	IV-B-1
shi	**sh**	97-98 ; 105	XIX-C-1a ; XIX-D-7b
si	**sh**	97-98 ; 105	XIX-C-1a ; XIX-D-7b
sion	**shun**	96 ; 97-98	XIX-B-4a ; XIX-C-1a
	zhun	96	XIX-B-4b
sive	**siv**	92	XIX-A-12
squ	**skw**	75-76	XVII-D-1

Letter	Sound	Page	Section
squa	skwo	27-28 ; 75-76	VII-A-2 ; XVII-D-1
ss	s	9-10	IV-A-1, 2
stle	sul	109	XX-A-6
sten	sun	109	XX-A-6
sub	sub	79	XVIII-B-7
sure	zhur	89	XIX-A-2
swa	swo	27-28	VII-A-2

Letter	Sound	Page	Section
t	t	1-2	I-B
	silent	109	XX-A-6
tain	tān	95	XIX-B-3a
	tun	95	XIX-B-3b
tch	ch	109	XX-A-6
th	th	13	V-A-1
	Th	13	V-A-1
ti	ti	103	XIX-D-6a
	sh	97-98 ; 104 ; 105	XIX-C-1a ; XIX-D-6b(1) ; XIX-D-7b
	ch	103-104	XIX-D-6b
tial	shul	90-91	XIX-A-6
	chul	90-91	XIX-A-6
tiate	shēāt	104	XIX-D-6b(1)(a)
tion	shun	96 ; 97-98	XIX-B-5a ; XIX-C-1a
	chun	96-97	XIX-B-5b
tious	shus	91	XIX-A-9
tive	tiv	92	XIX-A-13
trans	trans	80	XVIII-B-8
tt	t	10	IV-A-2
tu	tōo	102	XIX-D-5a
	chōo	102-103	XIX-D-5b

Letter	Sound	Page	Section
tur	**chur**	90 ; 103	XIX-A-3 ; XIX-D-5b(1)
ture	**chur**	90 ; 103	XIX-A-3 ; XIX-D-5b(1)

Letter	Sound	Page	Section
u	**u**	3-5 ; 43	II-A, B ; X-F
	ū	41 , 43	X-A, F
	o͞o	43	X-F-1
u . . e	**o͞o**	36-39	IX-A-1, B, C-1, 2, 3, 4
	ū	36-39	IX-A-1, B, C-1, 2, 4, 5
ue	**o͞o**	32 ; 99	VIII-C ; XIX-D-2a
	ū	32 ; 99-100	VIII-C-1 ; XIX-D-2b
	silent	100	XIX-D-2c
ui	**i**	34	VIII-F-1
	o͞o	34	VIII-F-2
	(o͞o, i)	34	VIII-F-2
ul(l)	**ul**	57	XIV-A
un	**un**	79	XVIII-B-6
ur	**ur**	59-60	XIV-B-3, 4
	ūr	60	XIV-B-3a, 4

Letter	Sound	Page	Section
v	**v**	1-2	I-B

Letter	Sound	Page	Section
w	**w**	2	I-C
	silent	108	XX-A-5
wa	**wo**	27-28	VII-A-2
war	**wōr**	65	XIV-C-1b
wh	**hw**	14	V-C-1
	h	14 ; 108	V-C-2 ; XX-A-5
wor	**wur**	62	XIV-B-5a(1)
wr	**r**	108	XX-A-5

Letter	Sound	Page	Section
x	ks	1	I-A
y	y	2 ; 45	I-C ; XI-A
	ē	9-10 ; 39 ; 45	IV-A-2 ; IX-C-3 ; XI-B-1
	ī	46 ; 47	XI-B-2 ; XI-C-2
	i	46	XI-C-1
ye	ī	46	XI-B-2
z	z	1-2	I-B
zz	z	9-10	IV-A-1, 2

INDEX

Selected Reading Rules

	Page	Section
Sound of consonant double-letter	9 ; 38	IV-A ; IX-C
General rule on short sounds of letter *a*	28-29	VII-A-3
Sounds of letters *al* and *all*	27-28	VII-A-2, 2a
General rule on short sounds of letter *o*	29	VII-B-2
Long sound of vowel letter and silent letter *e*	35	IX-A
Long sound of vowel letter with single consonant letter and specific endings	38	IX-C
General rule on sounds of single vowel letter	41	X
Sound of letter *e* at end of short word	41	X-B
Sound of letter *o* at end of word	42	X-C
General rule on sounds of letters *er, ir,* and *ur*	60	XIV-B-4

INDEX

Supplementary Spelling Rules

	Page	Section
Spelling of sound **k**	8 ; 11	III-A-2 ; IV-B-2
Doubling consonant letter at end of word	9	IV-A-1
Letters *q* and *u*	11	IV-B-3
Spellings *al* and *all*	28	VII-A-2
Doubling final consonant letter to keep vowel sound short	40	IX-C-5
Dropping silent letter *e* before adding *ing* or *y*	40	IX-C-5
Changing letter *y* to *i* before adding *es* or *ed*	53	XIII-B-2

INDEX

Selected Word Lists

	Page	Section
Consonant—short vowel—consonant words	4-5	II-B-1
Some initial sight words	5-6	II-D-2
Some consonant letter-sound combinations with		
Single short vowel sounds		
at *end* of words	19-21	VI-A-1, 2
at *beginning* of words	21-24	VI-B-1, 2
and *ing* ending	24-25	VI-C-1
with *consonant double-letters* and *ing*	25	VI-C-1a
and *ed* ending	25-26	VI-C-2
with *consonant double letters* and *ed*	26	VI-C-2a
Short vowel sound words changed to long vowel		
sound words by adding silent letter *e*	37-38	IX-B
Some long vowel sound words		
with *ing* ending	38	IX-C-1
with *ed* ending	38-39	IX-C-2
with *y* ending	39	IX-C-3
with *er* ending	39	IX-C-4
with *lc* ending	39	IX-C-5
Some words pronounced the same but spelled differently		
Same long sound vowel	69-70	XVI-A
Same short sound vowel	70	XVI-A
Other	71	XVI-A
Involving silent letters	110	XX-C
Some examples of words spelled the same but		
pronounced differently	71	XVI-B
Some common words and some irregular words	111-113	XXI-A, B

LETTERS
AND
SOUNDS

1

SINGLE LETTER — Single Consonant Sound

The first thing to do is teach the child all the single consonant letter-sound relations. These single consonant letter-sound relations are conveniently taught in three subgroups (adapted from Engelmann, 1966). If the child already knows the *names* of the letters in the alphabet, the letter-sound relations in each of the first two subgroups can be taught so as to take advantage of this. It is not necessary of course to teach the single consonant letter-sound relations in this way. And if it is not helpful for a particular child, they should be taught individually or in some other reasonable way.

A. *1st subgroup:* The name of each of these letters starts with a short vowel sound and ends with a consonant sound. The rule is: *To get the sound of the letter, drop the first part of the letter name.* (Note that the letter names have been transcribed in pronunciation symbols.)

Letter	Name of Letter	Sound of Letter
f	ef	**f** as in *f*at
l	el	**l** as in *l*og
m	em	**m** as in *m*at
n	en	**n** as in *n*ag
r	or	**r** as in *r*ag
s	es	**s** as in *s*at
x	eks	**ks** as in a*x*

B. *2nd subgroup:* The name of each of these letters starts with a consonant sound and ends with a long vowel sound. The rule is: *To get the sound of the letter, drop the final part of the letter name.*

Letter	Name of Letter	Sound of Letter
b	bē	**b** as in *b*at
d	dē	**d** as in *d*og
p	pē	**p** as in *p*at
t	tē	**t** as in *t*ag
v	vē	**v** as in *v*at
z	zē	**z** as in *z*ag
j	jā	**j** as in *j*og
k	kā	**k** as in *k*it

C. *3rd subgroup:* These letters are exceptions. You can't get the sound of the letter from its name.

Letter	Name of Letter	Sound of Letter
h	āch	**h** as in *h*at
w	dublū	**w** as in *w*et
y	wī	**y** as in *y*et

II

SINGLE LETTER — Single Short Vowel Sound

A. The next thing to do is teach the child the following single letter-single short vowel sound relations. The differences among the sounds involved in these relations—particularly those among the short vowel sounds **a**, **e** and **i**—are very difficult to hear and to utter on demand, even for a well-practiced adult. Each of the sounds is produced with the mouth open and all of them are quite similar. Before a child reaches a point where he can utter each sound in combination with various consonant sounds in a reliably differentiated way, he may literally have heard and produced them upon demand thousands of times. Discrimination among the single vowel letters is established relatively easily; it's establishing *reliable differentiation* among the associated vowel *sounds* that's hard for the child and takes him time.

Letter	Name of Letter	Short Sound
a	ā	**a** as in b*a*g
e	ē	**e** as in b*e*g
i	ī	**i** as in b*i*g
o	ō	**o** as in b*o*g
u	ū	**u** as in b*u*g

Note that we do not want to make the mistake of telling the child that, "The letter *a* makes the short vowel sound **a**," or that, "The letter *o* makes the short vowel sound **o**." If we made this seemingly simple error, and failed to correct it, the child is bound to be confused later when he is presented with the single short vowel letter-sound relations of the letter *a* and the sounds **o** and **u**, and the letter *o* and the sound **u**.

To avoid confusion later it is best to start by telling the child that the letters *a, e, i, o u* are called *Vowel Letters*. Next, that now he is going to learn some *Short Sounds* for these letters. And next, that these short sounds also are called *Short Vowel Sounds*. Then, explain that:

The short ā sound is **a** for the letter *a*.
The short ē sound is **e** for the letter *e*.
The short ī sound is **i** for the letter *i*.
The short ō sound is **o** for the letter *o*.
The short ū sound is **u** for the letter *u*.

Most children also find that it is easier to master these short vowel letter-sound relations if the letters and sounds are tied into a set of words. That is, they find it helps them to hear and to produce the different short sounds if they can use a set of words like "bag, beg, big, bog, bug" as a "memory aid."

B. Depending upon the discriminations and skills already acquired by a child, these single short vowel letter-sound relations could be taught right after the *1st subgroup* of single consonant letter-sound relations. If this is possible, the child can be started on *reading* words formed with the *1st subgroup* consonant and short vowel letters and sounds. The easiest pattern of words for him to start with should be that which follows the Consonant-Short Vowel-Consonant (CVC) pattern. Accordingly, he can be led step-by-step through matrices of CVC words and then started on reading simple sentences constructed with these words.

1. Matrices of CVC words can be made up as follows:

Nine word matrix: *1st subgroup*

ran	ran	ran
fin	fin	fin
run	run	run

or

fan	sin	fan
run	fan	run
sin	run	sin

Similar matrices can be constructed using only the *2nd subgroup* or consonants from the different groups. The following lists have been assembled for your convenience, and fairly well exhaust the various CVC combinations.

1st				*2nd*					
fan	man	ram	sin	bad	bat	dab	jet	pep	tab
fin	men	rim	sun	bed	bet	Deb	jot	pop	tub

fun	mom	rum	sis		bid	bit	dub	jut	pup	Tod
fix	mix	ran	sax		bud	bot	dad	kid	pat	Ted
fox	Mel	run	sox		bib	but	did	kit	pet	tap
lam	Nan	Rex	six		Bob	Bev	dud	pub	pit	tip
lax	nun	Sam			bub	dot	jab	pad	pot	top
lox	nil	sum			bop	dip	job	pod	tot	vat
										vet

1st & 2nd

bam	Dan	Jan	lap	mad	nap	pal	rap	sad	tan
bum	den	Kim	lip	mid	nip	Pam	rip	Sid	ton
ban	din	Ken	lop	mod	net	pox	sib	sod	tin
Ben	fad	lab	let	mud	not	rib	sob	sat	tun
bin	fed	lob	lit	map	nut	rob	sub	set	tax
bun	fat	lad	lot	mop	pan	rub	sap	sit	tux
box	fit	led	mob	nab	pen	rat	sip	sot	vim
dam	jam	lid	mat	nub	pin	rot	sop	Tim	van
dim	Jim	Liz	met	nod	pun	rut	sup	Tom	vex

1st & 3rd

ham	web	yam
hem	win	yum
him	wet	yen
hum	wit	yes
Hal	wed	yet
hen	wax	
has	yap	
his	yep	
hex	yip	

2nd & 3rd

had	hub
hid	hat
hod	hit
hip	hot
hop	hut

Obviously the words in a matrix must be rearranged periodically so that mere position of the word in a matrix does not control the correct response. Particularly at first matrices also should be constructed so that the words in them are fairly different in sound and appearance. With many children it pays to point out as well that whenever letter arrangements are the same, then the words are the same.

2. To increase the range of possible simple sentences you can construct for the child to read, it will help to teach him at this point a few *Short Vowel-Consonant* words and a small number of *"Sight"* words. Note that the following *Short Vowel-Consonant* words involve only letter-sound relations that have already been presented, so there is nothing irregular about the words:

am	if	on
an	in	up
at	is	us
	it	

While some of the following words also are quite regular in their letter-sound relations, they depart from a simple V-C or CVC pattern or involve relationships that have not been introduced yet. They are best taught at this point therefore as "Sight" words:

a	and	by	he	said	their	very	was
the	ask	gone	me	saw	them		want
I	any	put	she	say			
you	are		we	see			

Finally, it should be noted that we have left out a number of CVC, CV, and VC words from the various lists presented in this section. The reason for this is simple. Most of the CVC, CV, and VC words omitted involve additional letter and vowel sound relations which have not been presented yet. Thus, if for any reason there comes a point where the child needs to know one of the following words, it can be presented as a "Sight" word:

be	one	do	ah	law	bar	her	or
hi	won	to	ba	jaw	car	fir	for
	(was)	dew	ha	naw	far	mir	nor
	son	Jew	ma	paw	jar	sir	war
	ton	new	pa	raw	mar	cur	
	of	few	bah	(saw)	par	fur	
		mew	rah	yaw	tar		
		hew					

oh	bow	bow	bay	may	coy	key
go	low	cow	day	nay	boy	buy
ho	mow	how	gay	pay	goy	guy
lo	row	now	hay	ray	joy	hey
no	sow	pow	Jay	(say)	Roy	
so	tow	sow	Kay	way	soy	
yo	sew	vow	lay		toy	
		wow				

SINGLE LETTER — Two Consonant Sounds

Tell the child that for some letters we can say two sounds. And that now we are going to find out when to say one of two sounds for a *single* letter.

A. Tell him that for the letter *c* we say the sound **k** as in *c*at and the sound **s** as in *c*ent. Tell him, and illustrate for him, that the sound **k** is just the same as the sound we say when we see the letter *k*. Then tell him, and illustrate for him, that the sound **s** is just the same as the sound we say when we see the letter *s*.

1. Explain that usually when we see the letter *c* we say the sound **k** as in *c*at.

ca . .	*co* . .	*cu* . .	*cl* . .	*cr* . .
cat	cot	cut	clam	crab
can	cod	cud	clap	crap
cab	cob	cub	club	crank
cap	cop	cup	clip	crust

2. But when we see the letter *c* followed by the letter *e* or *i*, we say the sound **s** as in *c*ent. (Note that the letter-sound relations of *y* have not been introduced yet. So we do not present the letter-sound relation of *cy* here.)

ce . .	*ci* . .	. . *ce*
cent	cinder	dance
census	circus	since
center	citrus	prince
Certs	circle	trance

Spelling Rule: Before the short sound vowel letters *a, o,* and *u* the sound **k** is spelled with a letter *c*: cat, cob, cub. *Before* the short sound vowel letters *e* and *i,* it is spelled with a letter *k*: keg, kept, kit, king.

B. Tell the child that for the letter *g* we say the sound **g** as in *g*ot and the sound **j** as in *g*em. Tell him, and illustrate for him, that the sound **j** is just the same as the sound we say when we see the letter *j*.

1. Explain that usually when we see the letter *g* we say the sound **g** as in *g*ot.

g . .				. . *g*				
gag	gam	gas	bag	hug	jug	mug	sag
gab	gum	Gus	beg	hag	keg	nag	tag
gob	gun	gat	big	hog	lag	peg	tug
gad	gap	got	bog	hug	leg	pig	wag
God	gop	gut	bug	jag	log	rag	wig
			dig	jig	lug	rig	zag
			dug	jog	Meg	rug	zig

2. Next, explain that usually when we see the letter *g* followed by the letter *e* or *i* we say the sound **j** as in *g*em. But if the word doesn't make sense, then we say the sound **g**.

j		**g**
gem	gin	get
gent	ginger	git
germ	general	gift

3. Later, when the *long sounds* of the vowel letters are presented, point out **j** sound of the letter *g* in, for example:

j	
age	rage
cage	sage
page	wage

TWO LETTER SPELLING—
Single Consonant Sound

Once a child has begun to master what already has been presented, the letter-sound relations of this section can be introduced. Here as elsewhere the emphasis should be on both *letter-sound relations* and *words*, and what is consistent about them.

A. Explain that when we see two of the same consonant letters together we say just one sound for them. Also explain that we *always* say *short sounds* of *vowel letters* that come before two consonant letters.

1. Have the child read short words that *end* with the letters *ff, ll, ss,* and *zz*.

ff				*ll*		
buff	off	bell	sell	ill	kill	bull
cuff	doff	cell	tell	bill	mill	dull
huff	jiff	fell	well	fill	pill	full
puff	miff	jell	yell	hill	will	pull

zz				ss		
jazz	buzz	lass	Bess	hiss	boss	cuss
razz	fuzz	mass	less	kiss	loss	fuss
fizz		pass	mess	miss	toss	muss

Spelling Rule: In *most* short words *ending* with the sound of **f, l, s,** or **z** we double the last letter.

2. Next, have the child read such words as the following. Most children think that these words are fun to say and most of the words are familiar to them. At this point, merely tell the child that in reading

these words we say the sound $\bar{e}$ when we see the letter *y* at the *end* of the word.

bb	*dd*	*ff*	*gg*	*ll*		*mm*
gabby	daddy	daffy	baggy	Sally	silly	Sammy
Debby	Teddy	taffy	piggy	rally	dolly	Jimmy
Libby	kiddy	jiffy	doggy	belly	golly	mommy
Bobby	buddy	huffy	foggy	jelly	jolly	dummy
tubby	muddy	puffy	buggy	Billy	bully	yummy

nn	*pp*	*rr*	*ss*	*tt*	*zz*
Danny	happy	Jerry	sassy	fatty	jazzy
penny	peppy	merry	messy	Betty	dizzy
tinny	hippy	sorry	sissy	kitty	fizzy
bonny	poppy	furry	bossy	potty	tizzy
funny	puppy	hurry	fussy	nutty	fuzzy

3.   Some children also will have little difficulty reading the following words at this stage. This will be true even when the word is a "big" one or the child does not know what it means. At this point, a given child may well be excited by his correctly reading a "big" and textually "unfamiliar" word for the first time. Note that only words have been listed which involve the consonant letter-sound relations and the short sounds of the vowel letters presented so far.

add	Matt	egg	Ellis	eggshell
odd	mitt	burr	Ellen	bulldog
Ann	mutt	purr	uphill	bullfrog
inn	putt	offer	illness	hubbub

lessen	gossip	attic	cannot	erratic
unless	actress	mitten	cannon	current
dismiss	address	bottom	bonnet	interrupt
discuss	goddess	common	tennis	embarrass

B.   There are four other two-letter spellings that could be taught at this point: *sh, ck, qu, ph.* However, only *sh* and *ck* occur frequently with the short sound of a vowel letter in words. Since *qu* and *ph* occur almost entirely with other vowel sounds, it is best to just briefly present them to the child at this stage and postpone any major teaching of them until later.

1. Explain that when we see the letters *sh* together we say the sound **sh** as in *sh*op.

sh . . .		. . *sh*	
shag	ship	ash	dish
shop	shin	bash	fish
shot	shed	dash	mush
shod	shun	rash	gosh

2. Explain that when we see the letters *ck* together we say the sound **k** as in si*ck*; and that this is just like the sound we say for the letter *k*. For now, also tell the child that the letters *ck usually* come at the end of short words right after a vowel letter that has a short sound.

ack	*eck*	*ick*	*ock*	*uck*
back	deck	kick	dock	duck
rack	neck	nick	rock	puck
pack	peck	pick	lock	luck
sack	heck	sick	sock	suck

Spelling Rule: After a short sound vowel letter the sound **k** is usually spelled *ck*.

3. Explain that when we see the letters *qu* together we say the sound **kw** as in *qu*it.

qu . .
quit
quiz
quack
quick

Spelling Rule: The letter *q* is always followed by the letter *u* in a word.

4. Explain that when we see the letter *p* we say the sound **p**, and when we see the letter *h* we say the sound **h**. But, when we see the letters *ph* together we say the sound **f** as in *Ph*ilip. And this is just like the sound we say when we see the letter *f*.

TWO LETTER SPELLING—
Two Consonant Sounds

Tell the child that now he is going to find out about some more letters that we say two sounds for. Only this time it's when we see two letters together that we say these sounds.

A. Tell him that there are two sounds we say for the letters *th*, and the two sounds are almost the same.

1. Explain that when we see the letters *th* together in a word we say either a "hard" sound **th** as in *th*ick or a "soft" sound **Th** as in *th*en. Say the hard sound first. If the word doesn't make sense, then say the soft sound.

"Hard"		"Soft"	
th . .	. . *th*	. . *th*	. . *th*
thank thing	moth bath	than them	with (or "hard")
think theft	cloth path	that this	rather
thick throb	broth math	then thus	lather

B. Tell him that there are two sounds we say for the letters *ch*, but he only needs to remember one for now.

1. Explain that when we see the letters *ch* together we say the sound **ch** as in *ch*op.

ch . .			. . *ch*			
chat	chug	chick	ranch	bunch	punch	flinch
chop	chest	champ	bench	hunch	branch	crunch
chip	chill	chant	cinch	lunch	french	detach
			pinch	munch	trench	(which)

2. If the word doesn't make sense when we say the sound **ch**, then we say the sound **k** as in *ch*emist. This is the same sound we say for the letter *k*. Tell the child that most of the words where we say **k** for the letters *ch* are "big" words that he won't see very often in his reading at this point.

ch . .	*. . ch . .*
chasm	mechanic
chemist	technical
chronic	

C. Tell him that there are two sounds we say for the letters *wh*, but he really only needs to remember one.

1. Explain that when we see the letters *wh* together we say the sound **hw** as in *whack*.

wh . .
whack
whip
when
whisker

2. Then tell him that there are some words where we say just the sound **h** when we see the letters *wh*. But most of these words are "crazy" words (because of their vowel sounds) and we just learn them as "sight" words.

wh . .
who
whom
whose
whole

D. Since the letters *gh* occur most frequently with two letter vowel spellings, and vowel sounds other than short ones, it is best to just briefly present them at this stage and to postpone any major teaching of them until later.

1.   Explain that usually when we see the letters *gh* together in a word we say no sound—the letters are "silent."

Example: bou*gh*t

2.   But if we see the letters *gh* at the very beginning of a word or the word doesn't make sense when we say it, then we say the sound **g**.

Example: *gh*ost

E.   Tell him that there are two sounds we say for the letters *sc.* We say the sound **sk** as in *sc*at and the sound **s** as in *sc*ent. The sound **k** is the same as the sound we say for the letter *k* and the sound **s** is the same as the sound we say for the letter *s*.

1.   Explain that usually when we see the letters *sc* together in a word we say the sound **sk** as in *sc*at.

sc . .		*. . sc . .*
scat	scoff	rascal
scab	scum	discolor
scan	scurry	discover

2.   But when we see the letters *sc* together and they are followed by either the letters *e* or *i*, we say the sound **s** as in *sc*ent.

	sc	
scent	ascend	(discipline)
ascent	descend	(conscious)

F.   Tell him that there are two sounds we say for the letters *cc.* We say the sound **k** as in a*cc*ost and the sound **ks** as in a*cc*ent. The sound **k** is the same as the sound we say for the letter *k* and the sound **s** is the same as the sound we say for the letter *s*.
  Since most words involving the letters *cc* are fairly "big" words, and involve vowel sounds not yet presented, it is best to just briefly present them at this point.

1. Explain that usually when we see the letters *cc* together in a word we say just the sound **k** as in ac*cc*ost.

cc

accost
occult
moccasin
accomplish

2. But when we see the letters *cc* together and they are followed by either the letter *e* or *i*, we say the sound **ks** as in ac*cc*ent.

cc

accept
access
accident
eccentric

G. *Review:* At whatever point it looks like a child might find it most helpful the letter-sound relations of *c, cc, ck,* and *sc* can be reviewed and compared.

1. Point out that usually when we see the letters *c, cc,* and *ck* we say just the sound **k.**

c	cc	ck
cat	accost	back
cot	occult	rack
cut	accomplish	luck

2. But when the letters *c* and *cc* are followed by either the letter *e* or *i* we say the sound **s** and **ks**, respectively.

ce	ci	cce	cci
cent	citrus	accent	accident
center	cinder	eccentric	occident

3. And, when we see the letters *sc* together we usually say the sound

sk, but when they are followed by either the letter *e* or *i* we say just the sound **s**.

sc	*sce*	*sci*
scat	scent	(discipline)
scab	ascent	(conscious)

H.   Tell him that there are two sounds we say for the letters *ed* when we see them together at the *end* of a word, and the two sounds are almost the same.

1.   Explain that when we see the letters *ed* together at the end of some words we say just the sound **d** as in hang*ed*.

	. . . ed	
banged	nagged	jammed
hanged	sagged	pulled
robbed	gunned	yelled
sobbed	filled	buzzed

a.   But, if we see either the letter *d* or *t* before *ed* we say the sound **ud** as in land*ed* and rent*ed*.

. . ded		*. . ted*	
handed	acted	lasted	batted
landed	dented	rested	petted
sanded	rented	listed	pitted
mended	lifted	rusted	putted
padded	melted	busted	potted

2.   If the word doesn't make sense when we say the sound **d**, then we say the sound **t** as in bank*ed*.

		. . . ed		
asked	kicked	matched	passed	napped
banked	milked	patched	bossed	hopped
yanked	helped	jumped	tossed	dipped
thanked	gulped	pumped	missed	ripped

SOME CONSONANT LETTER—Sound Combinations with Single Short Vowel Sounds

The following lists of words involve single letter, two letter, and three letter consonant combinations. They should be helpful in teaching the child those combination sounds which occur frequently either at the beginning or the end of words. Taken individually, the letter-sound correspondences in the various beginnings and endings listed involve nothing that a child has not already encountered—assuming that he started at the beginning of the outline. The purpose here, however, is to present these beginnings and endings of words more as *units*. These units further emphasize the regularities involved in letter-sound relations as well as in reading in general.

A. At *End* of Words

Expanded lists of the words presented in this section can be found in Appendix X.

1. *Two Letters:* Assuming the child started at the beginning of the outline, the words in these lists already will be familiar or mastered. If so, they still can be reviewed with profit.

ab	ib	ob	ub		at	et	it	ot	ut
cab	bib	cob	cub		bat	bet	bit	bot	but
dab	rib	job	sub		cat	jet	fit	dot	nut
nab	fib	mob	tub		hat	pet	sit	lot	gut

ap	ip	op	up		ad	ed	id	od	ud
cap	hip	cop	cup		cad	bed	did	God	bud
lap	rip	hop	pup		bad	red	kid	mod	cud
nap	tip	pop	sup		sad	wed	rid	sod	mud

ax	ex	ox	*ix,* ux		ag	eg	ig	og	ug
ax	hex	box	mix		bag	beg	big	bog	bug
tax	sex	fox	six		rag	leg	dig	dog	hug
wax	vex	sox	tux		tag	peg	jig	log	tug

am	im	um	*em,* om		an	en	in	*on,* un
am	dim	bum	hem		an	den	fin	Don
ham	him	gum	Mom		can	men	pin	fun
jam	rim	sum	Tom		ran	ten	win	sun

2. *Three* Letters

ang	ing	ong	ung	ank	ink	*onk,* unk
bang	king	gong	hung	bank	ink	honk
gang	ring	long	rung	sank	mink	junk
sang	wing	song	sung	tank	pink	bunk
hang	sing	bong	lung	yank	sink	sunk

ant	ent	int	*ont,* unt	and	end	ond
ant	bent	hint	font	band	bend	bond
can't	cent	lint	bunt	land	send	fond
pant	tent	mint	punt	sand	lend	pond
rant	rent	tint	hunt	hand	mend	

ell	ill	oll	ull	ash	ush	*esh, ish,* osh
bell	bill	doll	bull	ash	gush	mesh
jell	pill	moll	full	dash	hush	dish
sell	kill	loll	mull	cash	lush	wish
tell	will		pull	mash	rush	gosh

ack	eck	ick	ock	uck	amp	ump	*emp, omp,* imp
back	deck	kick	dock	duck	camp	bump	hemp
jack	neck	lick	lock	luck	damp	dump	pomp
sack	heck	sick	sock	suck	ramp	pump	romp
pack	peck	pick	pock	puck	lamp	lump	limp

ast	est	ist	ost	ust	aft	ift	*uft, oft,* eft
cast	best	fist	cost	dust	raft	rift	tuft
fast	nest	gist	lost	must .	daft	gift	soft
past	pest	mist		just	Taft	lift	heft
last	rest	list		rust	waft	sift	left

atch	itch	*etch, otch,* utch
catch	itch	fetch
hatch	ditch	botch
match	pitch	Dutch
patch	witch	hutch

Some Additional *Three* Letter Endings: Short Vowel Plus-

-lt	-ct	-pt	-lf	-lk	-lm	-lp	-sk	-sp
belt	act	apt	elf	elk	elm	help	ask	gasp
melt	fact	rapt	self	milk	helm	kelp	mask	rasp
felt	pact	kept	golf	silk	film	gulp	desk	lisp
guilt	duct	wept	gulf	bulk		pulp	risk	wisp

B. At *Beginning* of Words

In the following lists we continue to use only the endings already presented in Section A.

1. *Two letters:* Since for most children it will be easier to read words which vary in their beginning but have a common ending, we have arranged the lists this way first. Then the lists are rearranged so that the beginnings are the same but the endings vary.

a. Different beginning and common ending. (Expanded lists of the words presented here also can be found in Appendix X.)

blab	glib	club	flat	flit	plot
flab	crib	flub	brat	slit	slot
slab	blob	grub	scat	grit	snot
crab	slob	drub	spat	spit	shot

grab	snob	stub	that	exit	spot
scab	swob	snub	chat	skit	shut

clap	clip	flop	flag	brig	slug
slap	flip	slop	brag	swig	drug
crap	slip	drop	drag	twig	smug
trap	drip	chop	snag	clog	snug
snap	trip	stop	shag	frog	thug
chap	ship	shop	stag	smog	chug

glad	slid	clod	clan	grin	glen
grad	grid	plod	plan	skin	then
bled	skid	prod	bran	spin	when
fled	crud	trod	Fran	twin	shun
sled	spud	shod	scan	thin	spun
shed			span	chin	stun

clam	slim	glum	clang	cling	clung
slam	grim	plum	slang	sling	slung
cram	trim	slum	whang	sting	stung
sham	skim	chum	Chang	bring	swung
swam	swim	drum	gang	thing	Chung
exam	whim	scum	hang	fling	flung

blank	blink	clunk	clamp	blimp	plump
plank	slink	slunk	cramp	skimp	slump
drank	drink	drunk	champ	chimp	chump
prank	brink	trunk	tramp	clomp	grump
spank	stink	skunk	scamp	stomp	thump
thank	think	chunk	stomp	chomp	stump

black	click	block	cluck	clash	blush
crack	slick	clock	pluck	flash	flush
track	trick	flock	truck	slash	slush
snack	brick	crock	snuck	crash	brush
shack	trick	shock	shuck	trash	crush
stack	stick	stock	stuck	smash	plush

plant	flint	snatch	sketch	smell	drill
slant	glint	thatch	blotch	shell	grill

chant	print	snitch	crotch	spell	skill
grant	blunt	switch	scotch	swell	spill
scant	grunt	twitch	clutch	skull	still
spent	stunt	which	crutch		chill

gland	craft	blast
brand	draft	chest
stand	theft	twist
blend	drift	crust
spend	shift	trust
blond	swift	frost

b. **Common beginning and different ending. (Expanded lists of the words presented here can be found in Appendix Y.)**

bl	*cl*	*fl*	*gl*	*pl*	*sl*
blob	clamp	flap	glob	plan	slap
blot	clasp	flesh	glad	plug	slam
blast	clash	flex	glum	plod	slob
blush	clot	flick	glop	plunk	slept
block	clip	flunk	glint	plant	slant
bled	club	flung	gland	plum	slop

br	*cr*	*dr*	*fr*	*gr*	*pr*	*tr*
brag	crab	drag	frank	grab	prank	trap
brat	crank	drank	fresh	grand	prop	tramp
brand	crust	drip	frisk	grip	prim	track
brig	crack	drift	frill	grub	prom	trim
bring	crept	drum	frock	grin	print	trust
brush	crisp	drunk	frost	grasp	prick	trunk

sc	*sk*	*sm*	*sn*	*sp*	*st*	*sw*
scab	skid	smack	snag	spank	stab	swam
scamp	skin	smash	snug	spin	stamp	swell
scan	skill	smell	snip	spot	still	swept
scant	skull	smelt	snub	spell	stunt	swift
scat	sketch	smut	snatch	spend	stung	switch
scum	skunk	smock	snuck	spunk	stuck	swung

ch	sh	th	wh	ex	qu	tw
champ	shag	thank	wham	exact	quack	twang
chat	shack	thick	whack	exam	quick	twist
chick	shed	think	when	exit	quit	twig
chill	shop	thing	whip	exist	quill	twin
chunk	shot	thin	whop	exult	quilt	twit
chump	shock	theft	whisk	(exotic)	quip	twitch

2. Three letters

spl	scr	shr	spr	str	thr	squ
splat	scrap	shrank	sprang	strap	thrash	squib
split	scram	shred	spring	strip	thresh	squid
splint	scrub	shrimp	sprung	strong	throb	squint
splash	scrimp	shrill	spred	strum	thrill	squish
splotch	scratch	shrink	sprint	stretch	thrift	

C. This also is a good place to introduce and review *ing* and *ed* as units at the *end* of words, and using only words already presented in this section.

1. One and two letter beginnings and *ing* ending.

banging	banking	panting	landing	dashing	backing
hanging	yanking	renting	sanding	gushing	kicking
ringing	inking	hinting	ending	dishing	locking
singing	honking	hunting	bending	wishing	ducking

lasting	camping	catching	lifting	helping	taxing
resting	limping	matching	melting	gulping	waxing
dusting	dumping	itching	acting	asking	foxing
rusting	pumping	pitching	milking	gasping	mixing

spanking	flashing	cracking	clamping	planting
thanking	crashing	clicking	stamping	chanting
blinking	blushing	blocking	chomping	glinting
drinking	brushing	trucking	slumping	grunting

snatching	blasting	drafting
switching	twisting	drifting
twitching	trusting	shifting
clutching	frosting	

a. With consonant double-letters.

jabbing	adding	nagging	selling	jamming
fibbing	wedding	gagging	telling	dimming
robbing	kidding	jogging	filling	gumming
sobbing	bedding	hugging	pulling	humming

canning	rapping	passing	batting	huffing
inning	sipping	missing	setting	puffing
winning	popping	bossing	hitting	razzing
running	topping	cussing	rotting	fizzing

blabbing	sniffing	bragging	chilling	cramming
crabbing	bluffing	dragging	drilling	slimming
grabbing	scuffing	slogging	smelling	swimming
snubbing	stuffing	slugging	spelling	drumming

snapping	blessing	chatting	planning
whipping	dressing	spitting	grinning
shopping	pressing	shutting	spinning
stopping	crossing	blotting	stunning

2. One and two letter beginnings and *ed* ending.

t

banked	cashed	backed	camped	hatched	taxed	helped
yanked	wished	pecked	limped	matched	waxed	gulped
inked	hushed	kicked	bumped	itched	foxed	milked
honked	rushed	locked	pumped	pitched	mixed	asked

tud			**d**	**dud**
lasted	rented	acted	banged	landed
rested	hinted	melted	hanged	sanded
dusted	bunted		ringed	ended
rusted	hunted		winged	mended

t

spanked	flashed	cracked	clamped	snatched
thanked	crashed	clicked	stamped	switched
slinked	blushed	blocked	chomped	twitched
clunked	brushed	shocked	stumped	clutched

tud

planted	blasted	crafted
chanted	twisted	drafted
glinted	trusted	drifted
grunted	frosted	shifted

a. *With consonant double-letters*

d   **dud**

gabbed	nagged	jelled	jammed	canned	jazzed	added
fibbed	gagged	filled	dimmed	fanned	razzed	padded
robbed	jogged	pulled	hummed	gunned	fizzed	kidded
sobbed	hugged	dulled	summed	sunned		

t   **tud**

rapped	huffed	passed	batted
tipped	puffed	missed	petted
hopped		bossed	jotted
topped		bussed	rotted

d

blabbed	bragged	chilled	crammed	planned
crabbed	dragged	drilled	skimmed	grinned
grabbed	slogged	smelled	trimmed	skinned
snubbed	slugged	spelled	drummed	stunned

t   **tud**

snapped	blessed	sniffed	chatted
whipped	dressed	scoffed	blotted
shopped	pressed	bluffed	plotted
stopped	crossed	stuffed	spotted

SINGLE LETTER—
Two or More Short Vowel Sounds

Start by telling the child that for two of the *Vowel Letters* we say more than one *Short Sound*. Finding out that we say three short sounds for the letter *a* and two for the letter *o* is usually a great help to a child. With some practice, words that might have been impossible to handle start to become smooth sailing for him. If he has fairly well mastered by now saying the five short sounds in combination with different consonant sounds, he should have no difficulty with these additional letter-sound relations.

A. Tell him that there are *three short sounds* that we say for the letter *a*.

1. Explain that we already have learned that when we see the letter *a* in some words we say the short sound **a** as in b*a*t. But in some words when we see the letter *a* we also say a short sound **u** that is like the short sound we say for the letter *u*. Most often we say this short sound **u** when we see the letter *a* at the *beginning* or *end* of some word.

u. .			. . u . .	. . u	
amiss	along	adult	what	America	data
amass	aloft	adopt	cadet	Anna	extra
amid	aslant	abrupt	banana	bandanna	stamina
amend	alert	abandon	amazon	banana	ultra
America	aghast	abolish	Brazil	Santa	plasma
among	afresh	aback	vanilla	vanilla	replica

2. Explain that in some words when we see the letter *a* we also say a short sound **o** that is like the short sound we say for the letter *o*. Most often we say this short sound **o** when we see the letters *l(l)* or *r after* the letter *a* or we see the letters *w, sw,* or *qu before* it. (Point out that in some words where the letter *a* is followed by the single letter *l* we don't really say a sound for the *l*.)

al		*all*			*ar*	
malt	walk	all	hall	bar	card	cart
salt	talk	ball	tall	car	hard	harp
bald	palm	call	wall	far	lard	dark
scald	calm	gall	wallet	jar	yard	park

wa		*swa*	*qua*	*squa*
watch	wad	swab	quad	squad
water	want	swan	quality	squash
watt	wand	swap	quantity	squat
wash	wasp	swat	qualm	squab

a.   Say that usually when we see the letters *al* or *all* together in a word we say the short sound **o** as in m*a*lt. But if the word doesn't make sense then we say the short sound **a** as in *A*l.

al

al	*all*
Al	shall
Alice	gallant
Alfred	gallon
album	gallop
alcohol	ballad

Spelling Rule: When the letters *al* are followed by a consonant letter we use just one *l*.

3.   Explain that for now our *General Rule* is: When we see the letter *a* in a word, and we are not sure what the word or sound is, we say the short sound **a** first. If the word doesn't make sense then we say the short sounds **u** and **o**.

What this means is that if the child sees the word "banana" and he first says **banana** we will not be surprised. Note, however, that this pronunciation is close to the so-called correct one and if the child now knows that often we say the short sounds **u** and **o** for the letter *a* he will, with a little practice, almost simultaneously re-say and recognize the word as **bunanu**. You will also find that many children with continued practice in reading, and more or less on their own, will end up "sluffing" or "muttering" the short sound **a** so that it sounds much like a short sound **u** or **o**. This is consistent with the *General Rule* presented above. And it often does, of course, help the child to say correctly and recognize a word.

The main reason why the *General Rule* presented here works is, of course, that taken together we say the short sounds **u** and **o** about twice as often as we say the short sound **a** for the letter *a* in words.

B. Tell him that there are *two short sounds* that we say for the letter *o*.

1. Explain that we already have learned that when we see the letter *o* in some words we say the short sound **o** as in h*o*t. But in some words when we see the letter *o* we also say a short sound **u** that is like the short sound we say for the letter *u*. Most often we say this short sound **u** when we see the letters *on*, *oth*, or *or* together in a word as in s*on*, m*oth*er, and w*or*d.

u

on		*oth*	*or*		"*Also*"
son	among	other	word	valor	cover
ton	lemon	another	worm	vapor	lover
won	wonder	brother	world	honor	governor
monk	sponge	mother	worst	minor	innocent
month	summon	smother	vigor	color	toboggan

(Later: honey, money, Monday, monkey, onion, tongue, none, done)

(Later: come, some)

2. Say that for now our *General Rule* is: When we see the letter *o* in a word, and we are not sure what the word or sound is, we say the short sound **o** first. If the word doesn't make sense then we say the short sound **u**.

VIII

TWO LETTER SPELLING —
One or More Vowel Sounds

Tell the child that now he is going to find out about some other letters that we say one or two *vowel sounds* for. This time it's when we see two letters together that we say these vowel sounds. Tell him that some of these vowel sounds are "new" ones that he hasn't practiced saying yet.

A. Explain that we have already learned that in some words when we see the letter *a* followed by the letters *l, ll,* or *r* we say a *short sound* that is like **o**. Then explain that usually when we see the letters *aw* or *au* together in a word we also say a short sound that is like **o**, as in s*aw* and h*au*l. Point out that the letters *aw* more often are at the *end* of a word and the letters *au* at the *beginning* or *inside* a word.

VIII

o

. . . aw			*. . aw .*	
jaw	claw		dawn	hawk
law	draw		fawn	squawk
paw	thaw		lawn	bawl
raw	straw		pawn	crawl
saw	squaw		yawn	brawl

au . . .			*. . au . .*		
August	haul	faucet	haunted	paunch
audit	Paul	saucer	jaunt	pauper
author	maul	cause	taunt	saunter
autumn	fault	pause	launder	flaunt
aunt(or **ant**)	vault	gauze	launch	fraud

B. Tell the child that usually when we see the letters *oo* together in a word we say either a long sound $\overline{oo}$ as in m*oo*n or a short sound **oo** as in b*oo*k.

1. Explain that we say the long sound $\overline{oo}$ first.

$$\overline{oo}$$

boo	food	fool	room	moon	droop	goose	boot	ooze
coo	mood	pool	bloom	noon	scoop	loose	hoot	choose
moo	brood	tool	broom	soon	sloop	moose	root	pooper
too	goof	spool	gloom	spoon	snoop	noose	toot	blooper
zoo	roof	stool	groom	swoon	stoop	boost	scoot	bamboo
	proof	school	boon	coop	swoop	roost	shoot	cartoon
	spoof	spook	coon	hoop	troop	booth	snoot	schooner
	cool	boom	goon	loop	whoop	tooth	spoor	Snoopy

2. If the word doesn't make sense then we say the short sound oo. (*Subrule:* When we see the letter *k after* the letters *oo* we usually say oo.)

oo

book	took	good	hoof
cook	brook	hood	foot
hook	crook	wood	soot
look	shook	stood	wool

C. Explain that usually when we see the letters *ew* or *ue* together in a word we also say a long sound $\overline{oo}$, as in dr*ew* and bl*ue*.

. . . *ew*			. . . *ue*		
dew	flew	slew	due	clue	duel
Jew	brew	stew	rue	glue	grueling
new	crew	screw	sue	true	gruesome
chew	drew	shrew	blue	cruel	fluent
blew	grew	threw			

1. But, in a few words, we say a long sound $\bar{u}$, as in f*ew* and f*ue*l.

ew	*ue*
few	cue
mew	hue
spew	fuel

D. Explain that when we see the letters *oi* or *oy* together in a word we say the sound **oi**, as in b*oi*l and b*oy*. Point out that the letters *oi* more often are *inside* and the letters *oy* at the *end* of a word.

	. . *oi* . .			
oil	toil	joint	choice	voice
boil	spoil	point	loiter	anoint
coil	broil	hoist	avoid	sirloin
foil	coin	moist	toilet	turmoil
soil	join	poison	Detroit	noise

. . . *oy*		
boy	cloy	ahoy
coy	ploy	convoy
joy	employ	corduroy
Roy	enjoy	voyage
toy	destroy	loyal

E.   Tell him that there are two sounds we frequently say for the letters *ou* ; the sound **ow** and the short sound **u**.

1.   Explain that usually when we see the letters *ou* together in a word we say the sound **ow**, as in *ou*t.

		. . *ou* . .			
out	our	bound	ouch	ounce	house
pout	hour	found	couch	bounce	louse
about	sour	hound	pouch	council	mouse
scout	flour	mound	crouch	count	blouse
shout	scour	pound	grouch	account	mouth
snout	loud	round	slouch	mount	south
spout	cloud	sound	foul	amount	devout
trout	proud	ground	(wound)	devour	

2.   If the word doesn't make sense when we say the sound **ow**, then we usually say a short sound **u**, as in c*ou*ple (Point out that this sound is like the short sound **u** we say when we see the letter *a, o,* or *u* in some words.)

	. . *ou* . .	
touch	couple	young
tough	double	Douglas
rough	trouble	carousel
cousin	doubloon	camouflage
country	bourbon	famous

3.   Point out that *less frequently* when we see the letters *ou* together in a word we say the long sound $\overline{oo}$, as in s*ou*p ; and even less frequently the long sound ō, as in c*ou*rt.

$\overline{oo}$		$\bar{o}$
you	soup	course
youth	coupon	court
tour	cougar	four
(wound)	croup	soul
(your)	group	(your)

4.   Finally, explain that if the letters *ou* are followed by the letters *ght* in a word we say a short sound **o** for the letters *ou* and the letters *gh* are "silent," as in *ou*ght.

. . ought

bought
brought
fought
sought
thought

F.   Tell him that there are two sounds we say for the letters *ui*; the short sound **i** and the long sound **$\overline{oo}$.**

1.   Explain that usually when we see the letters *ui* together in a word we say a single short sound **i**, as in b*ui*lt. (Point out that this is like the short sound **i** we say for the letter *i*.)

. ui . .

built	quiz	quit	biscuit
quilt	quick	quilt	circuit
guitar	quip	liquid	building

2.   If the word doesn't make sense when we say the sound **i**, then we usually say either a single long sound **$\overline{oo}$** or a long sound **$\overline{oo}$** and a short sound **i** separately, as in fr*ui*t and fl*ui*d.

$\overline{oo}$		$\overline{oo}$ and **i**	
fruit	bruise	fluid	ruin
suit	cruise	Bruin	suicide
juice	nuisance	Louis	tuition

IX

SINGLE LETTER AND "SILENT" e—
Single Long Vowel Sound

Remind the child that the letters *a, e, i, o, u* are called *Vowel Letters*, and that he already knows some *Short Sounds* for these letters.

Tell him that now he is going to find out about *Long Sounds* for these letters.

Explain that the *Long Sound* for each letter is simply the letter's name.

A.   Give him the *rule* that when we see one of the vowel letters and it is followed by a consonant letter and a letter *e* we say the long sound of the letter. Point out that the *e* letter is silent.

a . . e

jade	age	came	ape	cane	babe
wade	cage	fame	gape	Jane	safe
blade	page	game	tape	lane	strafe
grade	rage	name	drape	sane	stage
trade	sage	same	grape	wane	
shade	wage	tame	shape	crane	

ale	pale	ate	late	cave	wave	ace	brace
bale	sale	date	mate	Dave	slave	face	grace
Dale	tale	fate	rate	gave	brave	lace	trace
gale	whale	gate	crate	pave	crave	mace	place
hale	scale	hate	state	rave	grave	pace	space
male	shale	Kate	plate	save	shave	race	

daze	blaze	bake	rake	flake	base	⌈baste	mange⌉
faze	glaze	cake	sake	brake	case	haste	range
gaze	craze	fake	take	snake	vase	paste	change
haze	graze	lake	wake	shake	chase	⌊taste	strange⌋
maze	amaze	make	quake	stake			

e .. e

eve	Pete	recent
even	theme	decedent
Steve	scheme	athlete
Gene	recede	delete
scene	impede	complete

i .. e

dime	pipe	fire	bite	dive	life	vibe
lime	ripe	hire	kite	five	wife	bribe
time	wipe	dire	trite	hive	strife	scribe
crime	yipe	sire	spite	jive	rise	size
grime	swipe	tire	sprite	live	wise	prize
chime	stripe	wire	white	drive		

ride	slide	ice	rice	bike	Mike	line	brine	bile	rile
side	bride	dice	vice	dike	pike	mine	shine	file	tile
tide	pride	lice	slice	hike	spike	nine	swine	mile	wile
wide	snide	mice	spice	like	strike	vine	whine	pile	while
glide	stride	nice	twice						

o .. e

joke	broke	ore	more	shore	cove	clove	dome	robe	
poke	smoke	bore	pore	chore	hove	drove	home	probe	
woke	spoke	core	sore	snore	rove	stove	note	globe	
choke	stoke	fore	tore	swore	wove	strove	tote	doze	
bloke	stroke	gore	wore	store					

cole	pole	bone	drone	hope	grope	dose	chose	bode	
dole	role	lone	prone	nope	scope	hose	close	code	
hole	sole	tone	phone	mope	slope	pose	prose	rode	
mole	whole	zone		rope		rose	those	strode	

1. Explain that while it's true that the long sound of the letter *u* is *ū*, and that we say this sound in some words when we see the letter *u* followed by a consonant and a silent letter *e*, we more frequently say another sound. *Usually* when we see the letter *u* followed by a consonant and a silent letter *e* we say the sound $\overline{oo}$ as in r*u*le. If the word doesn't make sense *then* we say the long sound *ū* as in *use*.

u .. e

$\overline{oo}$					$\overline{u}$		
lube	nude	rule	yule		use	cure	cute

duke	rude	June	lure		fuse	pure	mute
juke	crude	tune	ruse		cube	sure	mule
Luke	prude	prune	brute		Jude	fume	puke

B.   Demonstrate how adding a silent *e* letter to a word changes the vowel sound we say from a short one to a long one, and how we thereby end up with a *different* or *new* word.

a

Short	Long	Short	Long	Short	Long	Short	Long	Short	Long
at	ate	can	cane	cap	cape	cam	came	fad	fade
bat	bate	ban	bane	gap	gape	dam	dame	mad	made
fat	fate	Jan	Jane	nap	nape	gam	game	glad	glade
gat	gate	man	mane	tap	tape	lam	lame	grad	grade
hat	hate	pan	pane	crap	crape	Sam	same		
mat	mate	plan	plane	scrap	scrape	blam	blame	rag	rage
pat	pate					sham	shame	sag	sage
rat	rate							wag	wage
plat	plate							stag	stage
slat	slate								

e

Short	Long
pet	Pete
them	theme

i

Short	Long	Short	Long	Short	Long	Short	Long	Short	Long
bit	bite	din	dine	pip	pipe	dim	dime	bid	bide
kit	kite	fin	fine	rip	ripe	Tim	time	hid	hide
sit	site	pin	pine	yip	yipe	slim	slime	rid	ride
quit	quite	win	wine	snip	snipe	grim	grime	slid	slide
writ	write	shin	shine	grip	gripe	prim	prime		
spit	spite	twin	twine	strip	stripe				

o

Short	Long	Short	Long	Short	Long	Short	Long
not	note	cod	code	lob	lobe	cop	cope
rot	rote	mod	mode	rob	robe	hop	hope
tot	tote	rod	rode	glob	globe	lop	lope
con	cone	nod	node			slop	slope

	u		
Short	*Long* ($\overline{oo}$)	*Short*	*Long* ($\bar{u}$)
rub	rube	cub	cube
tub	tube	cut	cute
dud	dude	hug	huge
crud	crude	us	use

C. Review and explain that when we see a *vowel letter* followed by a *consonant double-letter* we say a *short sound* for the vowel letter. Then explain that if the *vowel letter* is followed by a *single consonant letter* and the word ends in *ing, ed, y, er,* or *le* we say a *long sound* for the vowel letter.

1. Words ending in *ing*.

$\bar{a}$					$\bar{\imath}$		
fading	facing	baking	taping	icing	filing	chiming	hiring
wading	pacing	making	shaping	bribing	piling	shining	firing
caging	racing	taking	dating	riding	hiking	whining	tiring
naming	placing	waking	shaving	striding	liking	striving	wiring
taming	spacing	shaking	chasing	lining	wiping	driving	biting

$\bar{e}$	$\bar{o}$			$\overline{oo}$	$\bar{u}$
evening	coding	joking	hoping	tubing	using
scheming	poling	poking	roping	lubing	fusing
receding	roling	choking	groping	tuning	fuming
deleting	homing	toning	boring	pruning	puking
completing	toting	zoning	closing	ruling	curing

2. Words ending in *ed*.

$\bar{a}$					$\bar{\imath}$		
faded	faced	baked	taped	iced	filed	chimed	hired
waded	paced	faked	shaped	bribed	piled	shined	fired
caged	raced	quaked	dated	prided	hiked	whined	tired
named	placed	raked	shaved	glided	liked	strived	wired
tamed	spaced	staked	chased	lined	wiped	dived	piped

$\bar{e}$	$\bar{o}$			$\overline{oo}$	$\bar{u}$
schemed	coded	joked	hoped	tubed	used

38　　*Letters and Sounds*

decented	poled	poked	roped	lubed	fused
deleted	roled	choked	groped	tuned	fumed
completed	domed	toned	bored	pruned	cubed
receded	toted	zoned	closed	ruled	cured

3. Words ending in *y*. (For now merely remind the child that for the letter *y* at the end of these words we say the long sound **ē**.)

ā		ī	ō		o͞o
baby	Navy	Ivy	bony	cosy	ruby
lady	hazy	shiny	pony	roly	Judy
Sady	lazy	slimy	Sony	poly	Lucy
shady	crazy	grimy	stony	phony	jury

4. Words ending in *er*. (For now simply tell the child that for the letters *er* at the end of these words we say the sound **ur**.)

ā					ī			
paper	safer	baker	braver	danger	icer	miler	riper	diver
cager	wafer	faker	graver	manger	nicer	primer	diner	driver
wager	pacer	shaker	shaver	ranger	wider	hiker	finer	striver
tamer	racer	later	laser	changer	rider	striker	shiner	wiser
saner	trader	rater	chaser	stranger	glider	wiper	whiner	whiter

ē	ō			o͞o	ū
Peter	coder	joker	rover	cruder	user
meter	boner	poker	roper	tuner	fumer
schemer	loner	choker	closer	pruner	cuter
	sober	smoker	poser	ruler	surer

5. Words ending in *le*. (For now simply tell the child that for the letters *le* at the end of these words we say the sound **ul**. The letter *e* is silent.)

ā		ī		ū
able	ladle	Bible	rifle	bugle
cable	cradle	idle	trifle	
fable	maple	sidle	stifle	
sable	staple	bridle	title	
table	stable			

Spelling Rule: To keep the *vowel sound short* in words ending in *ing, ed, y, er* and *le, double* the *final consonant letter* before adding the ending.

Spelling Rule: For words that have a long sound vowel letter and end in silent *e,* drop the *e* before adding *ing* or *y.*

GENERAL RULE FOR SINGLE VOWEL LETTER—
Short or Long Sound

Tell the child that our *General Rule* will be that when we see a *single* vowel letter in a word, and we are not sure what the word or sound is, we say the *short sounds first*. If the word doesn't make sense then we say the *long sounds*.

A. Point out that most often we say a short sound when we see the single letter *a, e, i, o,* or *u* at the *beginning* of a word. But that at the *beginning* of some words we do say a long sound for these letters. (Note, however, that if a child says a short sound for the vowel letter at the beginning of some of the following words he will come close to a correct pronunciation of the word.)

a . . .	*e* . . .			*i* . . .
ache	eject	equal	evil	ivy
acre	elate	equip	evade	ivory
angel	Egypt	erase	event	idol
April	eleven	erect	ether	Irish
apron	elapse	emerge	eternal	isolate
apricot	elastic	emotion		identify

o . . .		*u* . . .
oh	omit	unit
odor	open	usual
obey	oval	utensil
okay	over	uniform
occur	order	universe
o'clock	Olympics	United States

B. Point out that when we see a *single* letter *e* at the *end* of a *short word* we usually say the long sound ē as in bᵉ.

```
. . e
be
he
me
we
she
```

C.   Point out that when we see the *single* letter *o* at the *end* of a word we usually say the long sound ō as in g*o*.

```
            . . . o

go    coco    hero    banjo
ho    dodo    zero    burro
lo    loco    auto    Idaho
no    solo    lotto   limbo
so    judo    motto   potato
pro   yoyo    hello   avocado
```

D.   Explain that when we see the letters *old*, *olt*, *oll*, or *ost* together in a word we usually say a long sound ō for the letter *o*, as in c*old,* b*olt,* r*oll,* and m*ost.*

	(Long)			
old		*olt*	*oll*	*ost*
old	hold	bolt	poll	host
bold	mold	colt	roll	most
cold	sold	jolt	toll	post
fold	told	molt	scroll	ghost
gold	scold	volt		

1.   But if the word doesn't make sense when we say ō for the letter *o* in *oll* and *ost* then we usually say a short sound o as in j*oll*y and l*ost.*

	(Short)		
oll		*ost*	
doll	holler-	cost	jostle
moll	pollen	lost	posture
jolly	volley	foster	roster
golly	rollick	hostile	hostage

E. Explain that when we see the letters *ind* together in a word we usually say a long sound ī for the letter *i* as in f*ind*.

(Long)

bind	rind	binder
find	(wind)	kindly
kind	blind	behind
mind	grind	rewind

1. But if the word doesn't make sense then we usually say a short sound i for the letter *i* as in sp*ind*le.

(Short)

(wind)	kindred	windy
cindor	kindling	window
hinder	hindrance	windmill
tinder	kindergarten	vindicate

F. Explain that when we see a single letter *u* in a word we usually first say a short sound u as in ad*u*lt. And then a long sound ū as in m*u*sic.

(Short u)			**(Long ū)**		
absurd	conduct	rumble	amusing	human	pupil
adult	disturb	suspect	circulate	humor	popular
bonus	instruct	study	deputy	manual	occupant
brush	public	trumpet	educate	music	regular

1. But if the word doesn't make sense then we usually say a long sound o͞o as in d*u*ty.

(Long o͞o)

duty	Judy	numeral	super
brutal	jubilant	rumor	truth
cuckoo	Honolulu	ruby	truly
exuberant	lunar	stupid	Yukon

SINGLE LETTER y—*Vowel Sounds*

Point out to the child that he already knows that when we see the letter *y* in some words we say the sound **y** as in *yet*. And that when we see the letter *y* at the end of some words we say the long sound **ē** as in *baby*.

Then point out to him that we also say some other sounds when we see the letter *y* in some words. And that now he is going to find out more about these sounds and when to say them.

A. Explain that when we see the letter *y* at the *beginning* of a word we usually say the sound **y** as in *yes*.

yak	yep	yip	you
yap	yet	yum	yore
yam	yes	yonder	York
yank	yell	yellow	your

B. Explain that when we see the letter *y* at the *end* of a word there are two other sounds we usually say.

1. Explain that when we see the letter *y* at the *end* of a *bigger* word we usually say a long sound **ē** as in *baby*. (Note that we say this sound whether the word has a long, a short, or some other sound for the vowel letter inside it.)

(Long)			(Short)				(Other)
baby	shiny	gory	gabby	jolly	dandy	lanky	noisy
lady	finally	glory	daddy	foggy	candy	panicky	pointy
Navy	ivory	forty	happy	sloppy	handy	celery	chewy
gravy	holy	frosty	silly	muddy	sandy	energy	cloudy
crazy	bony	rosy	jelly	buddy	chancy	enemy	moody
pastry	stony	duty	pretty	bully	fancy	empty	goody

(Short)

entry	pity	dingy	study
envy	fifty	stingy	gusty
every	sixty	sticky	sulky
frenzy	filthy	copy	murky
twenty	frisky	policy	ugly
jerky	windy	rocky	topsy-turvy

a. Point out, however, that when a word ends with the letters *fy* we say a long sound ī for the letter *y*.

fortify

mortify

identify

qualify

satisfy

2. But when we see the letter *y* or *ye* at the *end* of a *shorter* word we usually say a long sound ī, as in sk*y* and e*ye*.

by	sky	cry	wry	bye	(aye)
my	spy	dry	spry	dye	(buy)
fly	sty	fry	defy	eye	(guy)
ply	shy	pry	deny	lye	
sly	why	try		rye	

C. Explain that when we see the letter *y* inside a word we also usually say one of two sounds; either a short sound i as in lynch or a long sound ī as in type.

1. Explain that we say a short sound i first.

i

gyp	crystal	hypnotic	oxygen	sympathy
gypsy	cylinder	Lynn	Olympic	system
Egypt	cynic	lynch	pygmy	synagogue
gym	cyst	myth	Plymouth	syrup
gymnastic	dysentery	mystery		typical

2. If the word doesn't make sense then we say a long sound ī.

ī

asylum	dryness	hyena	rhyme
Byron	dyke	hydrant	style
cycle	dynamic	hydraulic	type
cyclist	dynamite	nylon	tyrant
cyclone	hybrid	python	typhoon

TWO LETTER SPELLING—
Single Long Vowel Sound

Finding out about the sound-letter relations covered in this and the next section often clears up a lot of confusion for a child and results in rapid improvement in his reading.

Tell him that the long vowel sounds $\bar{a}$, $\bar{e}$, and $\bar{o}$ are often spelled with *two* letters. And that now he is going to find out about these long vowel sounds and their two letter spellings.

A. Explain that usually when we see the letters *ai* or *ay* together in a word we say a long sound $\bar{a}$, as in m*ai*l and m*ay*. (The letters *i* and *y* are silent.) Point out that the letters *ai* are usually *inside* and the letters *ay* at the *end* of a word.

. ai . .							. . . ay		
maid	jail	flail	rain	Spain	taint		bay	nay	bray
paid	mail	frail	vain	sprain	quaint		day	pay	fray
raid	nail	snail	wain	stain	praise		Fay	ray	gray
laid	pail	trail	chain	strain	raise		gay	say	pray
braid	rail	braille	brain	train	bait		hay	way	tray
staid	sail	claim	drain	ain't	gait		Jay	clay	stay
bail	tail	gain	grain	faint	wait		Kay	flay	sway
fail	wail	main	plain	paint	trait		lay	play	spray
hail	quail	pain	slain	saint	waist		may	slay	stray

Miscellaneous						*Miscellaneous*		
aid	bailiff	raider	dainty	obtain	okay	astray	bayonet
ail	faith	raisin	daisy	contain	decay	ashtray	crayon
aim	mailman	prairie	gaily	maintain	relay	betray	layer
ailment	metermaid	sailing	brainy	entertain	replay	portray	maybe
aimless	jailer	assailant	rainy	exclaim	assay	Sunday	mayor
avail	sailor	unpaid	derail	explain	essay	Friday	payday
available	tailor	waitress	retail	champaign	X-ray	Thursday	payment
await	traitor	daily	detail	complaint	away	Saturday	playful

B. Explain that usually when we see the letters *ee* together in a word we say a long sound *ē*, as in r*ee*f.

... ee

bee	tee	tree	draftee
fee	wee	spree	coffee
gee	Zee	three	referee
hee	flee	agree	tepee
Lee	glee	degree	dungaree
see	free	decree	Cherokee

. . ee . .

deed	creed	reek	keel	seen	peep	deer	beet	tweet
feed	freed	seek	peel	teen	seep	jeer	feet	fleece
heed	greed	week	reel	green	weep	leer	meet	cheese
need	speed	cheek	wheel	preen	cheep	peer	fleet	peeve
reed	steed	sleek	steel	sheen	sleep	queer	sleet	sleeve
seed	beef	creek	deem	screen	creep	veer	greet	leech
weed	reef	Greek	seem	beep	sheep	cheer	sheet	speech
bleed	leek	eel	teem	deep	steep	sheer	skeet	screech
fleed	meek	feel	keen	Jeep	sweep	sneer	sweet	seethe
breed	peek	heel	queen	keep	beer	steer	street	teeth

Miscellaneous

agreed	breeze	teeter	engineer
exceed	freeze	tweezers	pioneer
feeble	sneeze	parakeet	volunteer
needle	wheeze	squeegee	gleem
wheedle	squeeze	Yankee	esteem
beetle	agreement	sixteen	redeem
beeswax	freedom	peevish	teeny

C. Explain that usually when we see the letters *oa* or *oe* together in a word we say a long sound *ō*, as in b*oa*t and t*oe*. (The letters *a* and *e* are silent.) Point out that the letters *oa* are usually *inside* and the letters *oe* at the *end* of a word.

. oa . .   . . . oe

goad	coal	groan	goat	loathe	loave		doe	woe
load	goal	soap	bloat	boast	cocoa		foe	oboe
road	shoal	oar	float	coast	whoa		hoe	floe
toad	foam	boar	gloat	roast	coax		Joe	goes
loaf	roam	soar	throat	toast	aboard		Moe	toes
soak	Joan	roar	coach	board	approach		toe	poem
cloak	loan	boat	poach	hoard	loafer			
croak	moan	coat	roach	coarse				

TWO LETTER SPELLING—Two Vowel Sounds

The sound-letter relations covered in this section often are among those that give a child the most difficulty. Finding out about them is usually very helpful to him.

Tell him that now he is going to find out about some other two letter spellings of vowel sounds. For these two letter spellings there are two sounds that we say.

A. Tell him that usually when we see the letters *ow* together in a word we say either the sound **ow** as in h*ow* or a long sound **ō** as in bl*ow*.

1.   Explain that we say the sound **ow** first.

ow

. . *ow*		. . *ow* .		
(bow)	(sow)	owl	prowl	clown
cow	vow	fowl	scowl	brown
how	wow	howl	crowd	crown
now	chow	jowl	down	drown
pow	plow	yowl	gown	frown
(row)	brow	growl	town	drowse

Miscellaneous

cowboy	power	towel	kowtow
cowhand	powder	bowel	powwow
cowbell	powerful	vowel	somehow
cower	tower	trowel	nowadays
coward	flower	rowdy	downhill
chowder	shower	drowsy	downstairs

2.   If the word doesn't make sense then we say a long sound **ō**.

ō

. . ow			*. . ow .*	
(bow)	tow	crow	owe	flown
low	blow	grow	own	grown
mow	flow	show	owner	shown
(row)	glow	snow	bowl	thrown
(sow)	slow	throw	blown	growth

Miscellaneous

bowler	crowbar	strowler	below
bowleg	rowboat	lawnmower	elbow
bowling	showboat	lowbr*ow*	shadow
lowly	showoff	snowpl*ow*	widow
slowly	stowaway	towrope	window

a. Point out that if the letters *ow* come *after* a *double consonant letter* then we usually say a long sound ō.

bellow	pillow	narrow
fellow	willow	harrow
mellow	gallows	sparrow
yellow	shallow	borrow
hollow	swallow	sorrow
billow	arrow	marshmallow

B. Tell him that usually when we see the letters *ie* together in a word we say a long sound ē as in th*ie*f or a long sound ī as in t*ie*.

1. Explain that we usually say a long sound ē when we see the letters *ie* together *inside* or at the *end* of a *larger* word.

ē

. . ie . .

chief	field	niece	fierce	wiener
thief	shield	piece	pierce	belief
brief	wield	spiel	priest	grieve
grief	yield	fiend	shriek	relieve

. . . ie

movie	Dixie	bodies	species	candied	carried
eerie	zombie	Rockies	mysteries	emptied	married

prairie	rookie	parties	jalopies	dirtied	jellied
Marie	cookies	pastries	hippies	studied	worried
pixie	goodies	series	hobbies	varied	hurried

2. Explain that we usually say a long sound ī when we see the letters *ie* together at the *end* of a *smaller* word.

ī

. . . ie

die	dies	flies	defies	vied	fried
lie	lies	spies	died	plied	pried
pie	pies	fries	lied	spied	tried
tie	ties	pries	pied	cried	defied
vie	cries	tries	tied	dried	denied

Spelling Rule: When there is a consonant letter before the letter *y* at the end of a word, change the *y* to *i* before adding *es* or *ed*.

C. Tell him that usually when we see the letters *ea* together in a word we say either a long sound ē as in s*ea*t or a short sound e as in sw*ea*t.

1. Explain that we say a long sound ē first.

ē

ea . .		*. . ea*
eat	eager	pea
each	eagle	sea
ease	East	tea
easy	Easter	flea
ear	Eastern	plea

. . ea .

beach	bead	meal	peak	streak	scream
peach	(lead)	real	weak	beam	stream
reach	(read)	scal	bleak	team	bean
teach	plead	zeal	creak	gleam	dean
bleach	leaf	steal	freak	cream	Jean
preach	deal	beak	sneak	dream	lean
breathe	heal	leak	speak	steam	mean

clean	hear	smear	tease	seat	weave
heap	near	spear	please	cheat	beast
leap	rear	stear	beat	wheat	feast
cheap	(tear)	beard	feat	cleat	least
dear	year	cease	heat	treat	yeast
fear	clear	crease	meat	heave	peace
gear	shear	grease	neat	leave	leash

Miscellaneous

beacon	heathen	really	weary	congeal
beagle	league	reason	dreary	ideal
beaver	meager	season	squeak	ordeal
beatnik	measles	treason	sleazy	decrease
beauty	peacock	weazel	appeal	disappear
feasible	peanut	treaty	appear	repeat
feature	queasy	treatment	conceal	retreat

2. If the word doesn't make sense then we say a short sound **e**.

e

. . ea .

dead	dread	deaf	swear	death
head	tread	bear	sweat	breadth
(lead)	stead	pear	threat	leant
(read)	spread	(tear)	breast	meant
bread	thread	wear	breath	dreamt

Miscellaneous

breakfast	peasant	treadle	feather	ahead
heaven	pleasant	treasure	leather	abreast
heavy	pleasure	health	weather	instead
meadow	ready	wealth	realm	retread
measure	steady	jealous	weapon	pageant

Note that there are a few "crazy" words where we say a long sound ā for the letters *ea*: br*ea*k, gr*ea*t, st*ea*k, y*ea*. These can be taught as "sight" words and/or as exceptions.

D. Tell him that usually when we see the letters *ei* or *ey* together in a word we say a long sound ē as in rec*ei*ve and k*ey* or a long sound ā as in v*ei*l and ob*ey*. (The letters *i* and *y* are silent.) Point out that the letters *ei* are usually *inside* and the letters *ey* at the *end* of a word.

1. Explain that we say a long sound ē first.

ē

	. ei . .			. . . ey	
ceiling	neither	deceive	key	honey	jockey
either	seize	perceive	donkey	money	kidney
geisha	seizure	receive	monkey	covey	nosey
leisure	weird	conceit	turkey	valley	whiskey
Neil	conceive	receipt			

2. If the word doesn't make sense then we say a long sound ā.

ā

	. ei . .			. . . ey
beige	veil	freight	hey	prey
feign	vein	heinous	they	convey
feint	eight	neighbor	obey	survey
rein	weight	reindeer		

TWO LETTER SPELLING—Vowel-Consonant Combination Sounds Involving *l* and *r*

Tell the child that now he is going to find out about the sounds we say when we see a vowel letter and a letter *l* or *r* together in a word. Finding out about these sound-letter relations should help to correct any difficulty the child may be having with them.

A. Explain that when we see the letters *al, el, il, ol, ul, ull,* or *le* together at the *end* of a word we usually say the single sound **ul.**

al		*el*		*il*
brutal	physical	camel	model	devil
cannibal	regal	cancel	nickel	council
capital	rural	counsel	panel	pencil
cardinal	sandal	drivel	parcel	peril
dial	trial	easel	swivel	stencil
fatal	vital	gospel	tunnel	vigil

ol	*ul*	*ull*	*le*		
Carol	consul	bull	baffle	cable	handle
idol	awful	dull	bubble	cackle	kettle
petrol	pitiful	full	buckle	candle	people
pistol	insult	pull	bugle	circle	possible
symbol	result	skull	bundle	eagle	mingle

B. Tell the child that there are two sounds we say for the letters *er, ir, ur,* and *or.*

1. Explain that usually when we see the letters *er* together *inside* and at the *end* of a word we say the sound **ur** as in term. (*Subrule:* Usually when the letters *er inside* a word are followed by a *consonant letter* we say the sound **ur.**)

Bert	Jersey	mercy	perhaps	sherbet
berserk	herb	merge	perk	stern
Certs	herd	nerve	permanent	term
certain	hermit	percent	persist	terminal
fern	Hertz	perch	person	termite
germ	kernel	percolate	pert	verbal
German	merchant	perfect	sermon	verge
jerk	mercury	perform	servant	verdict

. . er

her	butcher	danger	father	later	officer	simpler	tiger
after	butler	deliver	fender	launder	other	sister	transfer
alter	catcher	diaper	finger	letter	over	sliver	ulcer
anger	cancer	differ	gambler	manager	pitcher	spider	under
baker	center	dinner	gather	master	prisoner	splinter	usher
better	chapter	dresser	grocer	monster	rather	super	wander
bicker	composer	eager	hamper	mover	rooster	summer	water
blubber	consider	Easter	hunger	never	saucer	temper	weather
bother	conquer	enter	inner	number	scooter	thunder	whisker
boxer	cover	ever	jumper	offer	seller	tender	winter

Miscellaneous

advertise	battery	convert	general	jitters	operate
afternoon	beverage	detergent	govern	lantern	pattern
Albert	boomerang	emergency	guerilla	liberty	property
allergy	bravery	energy	hibernate	machinery	reverse
answer	camera	exercise	iceberg	maverick	several
assert	clerk	exert	interest	modern	shepherd
average	concern	expert	insert	mobster	veteran

a. But then explain that sometimes when we see the letters *er* together *inside* or towards the beginning of a word we say the sound **er** as in v*er*y. (*Subrule*: Usually when the letters *er* inside a word are *followed* by a *vowel letter* that is *pronounced* we say the sound **er**.)

. er . .

ceremony	ferry	kerosene	serenade
cherish	era	merit	sheriff
cherry	errand	merry	terrible
derelict	error	peril	territory
Gerald	herald	periscope	therapy
Jerry	heritage	perish	very

America imperil
cherub Sierra
clerical experiment

2. Explain that usually when we see the letters *ir* together in a word we also say the sound **ur**, as in b*ir*d. (*Subrule:* Usually when the letters *ir inside* a word are *followed* by a *consonant letter* we say the sound **ur**.)

. *ir* . .

bird	fir	mir	skirt	twirl
birch	firm	mirth	skirmish	third
birth	first	quirk	squirt	thirst
circle	flirt	sir	squirm	thirsty
circuit	gird	sirloin	squirrel	whir
circus	girth	shirk	stir	whirl
chirp	giraffe	smirk	stirrup	Virginia
dirt	direct	shirt	swirl	Irving

Miscellaneous

admiral birdseed
affirm birthday
aspirin confirm

a. But then explain that sometimes when we see the letters *ir* together at the beginning or inside a word we say the sound **ir** as in sp*ir*it. (*Subrule:* Usually when the letters *ir inside* a word are *followed* by a *vowel letter* that is *pronounced* we say the sound **ir**.)

. . *ir* . .

conspirator mirror
empirical spirit
miracle irritate

3. Explain that usually when we see the letters *ur* together in a word we also say the sound **ur**, as in b*ur*n. (*Subrule:* Usually when the letters *ur* are *followed* by a *consonant letter* we say the sound **ur**.)

burn	curse	furnish	lurk	surf	splurt
burp	curve	furniture	lurch	surge	turn
burden	current	further	murder	surgery	turf
burglar	curtain	gurgle	murky	surplus	turban
burst	curfew	hurl	murmur	surprise	turkey
blur	church	hurt	purge	surround	turnip
curb	churn	hurdle	purple	survive	turpentine
curd	durable	hurricane	purpose	slurp	turtle
curdle	during	hurray	purse	spurt	urban
curly	fur	hurry	rural	splurge	urgent

Miscellaneous

disturb	plural	hamburger
flurry	return	liverwurst
incur	sturdy	Saturday
occur	suburb	Thursday

a.   But then explain that sometimes when we see the letters *ur* together inside a word we say the sound **ūr**, as in f*ur*y. (*Subrule:* Usually when the letters *ur* are *followed* by a *pronounced vowel letter* we say the sound **ūr**.)

. . *ur* . .

fury	Huron
furious	purify
curiosity	luxury

4.   Tell the child our *General Rule* is that when we see the letters *er*, *ir*, or *ur* together in a word we usually say the sound **ur**. But if the word doesn't make sense then we usually say the sound **er** for the letters *er*, the sound **ir** for the letters *ir*, and the sound **ūr** for the letters *ur*. (Our *General Subrule* is that when the letters *er*, *ir*, or *ur* are followed by a consonant letter we usually say the sound **ur**. But if they are followed by a pronounced vowel letter then we usually say, respectively, the sounds **er**, **ir**, and **ūr**.)

5.   Explain that usually when we see the letters *or* together at the *beginning* or *inside* a word we say a long sound **ō** for the letter *o*, as in b*or*n.

or	Oregon
oral	organ
orange	organize
orbit	origin
order	original
orchestra	ornament

. or . .

born	chorus	forest	horror	porch	stork
border	dorm	forget	horrible	porter	storm
cord	Doris	forbid	lord	portable	torn
cork	for	forever	moral	porcupine	torch
corn	Ford	formal	moron	sort	torment
corner	fork	Gordon	morning	short	tornado
corporal	form	gorilla	North	snort	torpedo
correlate	fort	horn	normal	sport	torrent
correspond	force	horse	pork	scorch	thorn
corridor	forge	hornet	port	sworn	worn

Miscellaneous

absorb	comfort	export	record	category
according	discord	explorer	report	dormitory
adorable	distort	Florida	scorpion	exploratory
afford	divorce	import	snorkel	glory
assortment	decorate	important	support	laboratory
before	effort	platform	temporary	story
conform	escort	porridge	transport	victory

a. But then explain that usually when we see the letters *or* together at the *end* of a word we say the sound **ur**, as in act*or*.

. . . or

actor	competitor	favor	major	prior	senator
anchor	doctor	flavor	mayor	professor	spectator
ancestor	donor	glamor	minor	radiator	tractor
author	honor	humor	mirror	razor	tutor
alligator	editor	inventor	monitor	reflector	valor
bachelor	educator	janitor	motor	rigor	vapor
color	elevator	labor	odor	rumor	vigor
conductor	error	liquor	pastor	scissors	visitor

TWO LETTER SPELLING—Vowel-Consonant Combination Sounds   61

(1)   Point out that we also usually say the sound **ur** for the letters *or* when the letter *w* comes before them.

wor . .

word	worst
work	worth
worm	worry
world	worship

C.   Tell him that there are essentially three sounds we say for the letters *ar* and three for the letters *our*.

1.   Explain that usually when we see the letters *ar* together in a word we say a sound for the letter *a* that is like a short sound **o**, as in *ar*m.

ar . . .

arc	arbor	Argentina	artic
are	arch	argument	article
ark	archer	armor	artist
arm	ardent	army	Arthur
art	ardor	arsenal	artichoke

. ar . .

barb	card	carton	dart	garlic
Barbara	cardiac	cartoon	darling	garment
barber	cardinal	carve	farm	harbor
barbecue	carfare	charge	farce	hard
bargain	cargo	Charles	farther	hardly
bark	Carl	charm	garb	hark
barn	carnival	chart	garble	harm
barge	carpenter	charcoal	garbage	harmony
bartender	carpet	dark	garden	harness
barnyard	cart	darn	gargle	harp

harpoon	mark	parlor	spark	starve
harsh	market	part	sparkle	starving
harvest	marmalade	partake	sharp	tardy
lard	marsh	particular	smart	target
lark	marshall	partner	snarl	tarnish
large	marvel	party	sparse	tartar
marble	parcel	sarcasm	Spartan	varnish
march	parch	sardine	stark	varsity
Marge	pardon	scarf	start	yard
margarine	park	shark	startle	yarn

... ar

bar	tar	ajar
car	char	bazar
far	scar	cigar
jar	spar	guitar
mar	star	radar
par	afar	seminar

Miscellaneous

alarm	discard
apart	discharge
apartment	guard
bombard	regard
department	retard
disarm	safari

a.   Then explain that sometimes when we see the letters *ar* together in a word we say a sound for the letter *a* that is like either the short sound **u** as in buzz*ar*d or the short sound **e** as in sc*ar*ce.

(1)   Tell him that we most often say the sound **ur** when we see the letters *ar* or *ard* together at the *end* of a word. Give him the *rule* here that if we're not sure when we see the letters *ar* or *ard* at the end of a word, we say the sound **or** first. But if the word doesn't sound right then we say the sound **ur**. (Note that if we say the sound **or** rather than **ur** for the letters *ar* in many of the following words we come quite close to a correct and recognizable pronunciation of the word.)

... ar

altar	collar	liar	regular
beggar	cougar	lunar	similar
calendar	dollar	Oscar	solar
caterpillar	grammar	peculiar	sugar
cedar	hangar	polar	vinegar
cellar	Kangaroo	popular	vulgar

... ard

awkward	coward	hazard	orchard
backward	Edward	haphazard	Richard
blizzard	forward	inward	standard
buzzard	gizzard	mustard	wizard

(2) Tell him that we usually say the sound **er** when we see the letters *ar* and *arr* followed by a vowel letter, or by a letter *y* at the end of a word.

. ar . .

Arab	marathon	apparel	baron
asparagus	parachute	apparent	Sharon
caramel	paradise	parent	Carol
character	Sarah	(area)	Harold

Arizona	Paris	various
baritone	parish	hilarity
charity	rarity	comparison
clarify	tariff	aquarium

. arr . .

barracks	barrel	barricade	arrogant
narrate	barren	barrier	carrot
embarrass		carrier	parrot

. . . ary

Gary	arbitrary	imaginary	ordinary
Mary	canary	January	primary
nary	contrary	library	sanitary
scary	customary	military	temporary
vary	February	necessary	vocabulary

. . . arry

Barry	Larry
carry	marry
Harry	quarry

(a) Point out that if the word doesn't sound right when we say the sound **erē** for the letters *ary*, then we say the sound **urē** as in burgl*ary*.

boundary

burglary

Calvary

salary

summary

b. Explain that when the letters *qu* or *w* come before the letters *ar* we have an exception and we say the sound **ōr**, as in *qua*rt and *wa*r.

quar . .		*war . .*		
quarantine	war	wart	warrant	award
quarrel	ward	warden	warrior	dwarf
quart	warm	warmth	warpath	reward
quarter	warn	warfare	warship	swarm
quartet	warp	warble	warlock	thwart

c. Finally, explain that sometimes when we see the letters *ar* or *arr* together towards the *beginning* of a word we say separately an **u** sound for the *a* and a **r** sound for the letters *r* or *rr*, as in *a r*ise.

a rena	ca rouse	a rrange
a rise	ga rage	a rray
a roma	ma rine	a rrest
a rouse	pa rade	a rrive
a round	pa role	ba rrage
a rithmetic	pa ralysis	

2. Explain that when we see the letters *our* together in a word we say one of three sounds that we already know for the letters *ou*.

a. Point out that usually when we see the letters *our* together in a *bigger* word we say a short sound **u** for the letters *ou*, as in j*our*ney.

. our . .		*. . our .*	
bourbon	journey	adjourn	neighbour
courage	nourish	encourage	sojourn
courteous	tourney	flourish	scourge
journal	tournament		

b. But usually when we see the letters *our* together in a *shorter* word we say either the sound **ow** or the long sound **ō** for the letters *ou*, as in h*our* and y*our*.

(1) Our rule is that we say the sound **owr** first.

our	sour
dour	flour
hour	scour

(2) But if the word doesn't make sense then we say the sound **ōr**.

four	course	fourth
pour	court	mourn
your	gourd	source

THREE LETTER SPELLING—Vowel-Consonant Combination Sounds Involving *r*

The sound-letter relations covered in this section should further simplify a child's task in reading letter combinations involving *r*.

A. Tell him that there are several letter combinations involving *r* where we say the same sound **er.**

1. Explain that usually when we see the letters *air* or *are* together in a word we say the sound **er**, as in h*air* and c*are*.

. air .		. are .		
air	flair	bare	pare	scare
fair	stairs	care	rare	share
hair	fairly	dare	wares	snare
lair	fairy	fare	blare	spare
pair	hairy	hare	flare	stare
chair	dairy	mare	glare	square

Miscellaneous			*Miscellaneous*		
aircraft	affair	hairless	barely	parent	beware
airline	despair	chairlift	bareback	harem	compare
airmail	repair	chairman	careful	apparel	declare
airplane	unfair	stairway	carefree	apparent	fanfare
airport	wheelchair	prairie	farewell	aware	welfare

2. Review and explain that usually when we see the letters *arr* together in a word, or the letters *ar* followed by a pronounced vowel letter or letter *y*, we also say the sound **er**, as in c*arr*ot and b*ar*on.

	. arr .			. ar + .	
barrel	Barry		Arab	scary
carrier	carry		caramel	canary
carrot	Harry		paradise	January
parrot	Larry		charity	necessary
narrow	marry		baron	temporary

3.   Review and explain that usually when we see the letters *err* together in a word or the letters *er* followed by a pronounced vowel letter we also say the sound **er**, as in *err*or and m*er*it.

. err .	. er + .
errand	herald
error	merit
terrible	sheriff
territory	therapy

B.   Point out that there are three sounds we frequently say when we see the letters *ear* together in a word, and that one of these is also the sound **er**.

1.   Review and explain that usually when we see the letters *ear* together in a word we say the sound **ēr** (or **ir**), as in f*ear*.

hear	clear
near	smear
year	beard

2.   But if the word doesn't make sense then we say the sound **er**, as in b*ear*.

bear	bearing
pear	underwear
swear	swearing

3.   If the word still doesn't make sense then we say the sound **ur**, as in l*ear*n.

early	learn	search
earn	heard	research
earth	pearl	yearn

68   *Letters and Sounds*

XVI

SOME WORDS PRONOUNCED OR SPELLED THE SAME WAY

A good way to review various vowel and vowel-consonant sound and letter relations is to present word pairs that are spelled differently but pronounced the same way or pronounced differently but spelled the same way.

Most children find that the sound-letter relations involved in the words presented in this section are easy and fun to deal with. They readily discriminate the similarities and differences in the spelling or the sound of words when they are presented together, and they usually respond to the task as a challenging game.

For easy reference we have presented here word pairs illustrating all the different letter-sound combinations. Simply refer to this section, therefore, if word pairs illustrating a particular sound-letter relation are desired for review (or teaching).

A.   Some words that are pronounced the same but are spelled differently because they have a different meaning.

Long Sound Vowel

ā		ē		ī		ō		o͞o	
ai — a .. e		*ee — ea*		*ie—ye*		*o(+e) — oa*		*ew — ue*	
maid	made	flee	flea	die	dye	bored	board	blew	blue
ail	ale	see	sea	lie	lye	border	boarder	flew	flue(flu)
bail	bale	tee	tea			horse	hoarse	slew	slue
Gail	gale	reed	read			lone	loan	dew	due(do)
hail	hale	peek	peak			ore	oar(or)		
mail	male	week	weak			sore	soar		
pail	pale	creek	creak			rode	road		
sail	sale	heel	heal			Rome	roam		
tail	tale	peel	peal						
main	mane(Maine)	reel	real			*o(+e)—ow* *Continued on following page.*			
pain	pane	steel	steal			oh	owe		

XVI

ā		ē		ō	
ai — a..e		*ee — ea*		*o(+e) — ow*	
plain	plane	seem	seam	lo	low
vain	vane(vein)	teem	team	rose	rows
bait	bate	cheep	cheap	shone	shown
gait	gate	deer	dear		
maize	maze	sheer	shear	*o..e — ou*	
raise	raze	beet	beat	fore	four(for)
waist	waste	feet	feat	pore	pour(poor)
		meet	meat	sole	soul

(Also)		(Also)	
bee	be	so	sew
wee	we	role	roll
peer	pier	pole	poll
sees	seize	flow	floe
peace	piece	tow	toe
hear	here	towed	toad
		course	coarse

Short Sound Vowel

er		**e**		**o**	
air — are		*e — ea*		*a(ll)—aw(l)*	
fair	fare	led	lead	pa	paw
hair	hare	red	read	rah	raw
pair	pare	bred	bread	ball	bawl
flair	flare				

ear — are				*all — aul*	
bear	bare			hall	haul
pear	pare			mall	maul
wear	ware			pall	Paul

ar(r) — er(r)	
vary	very
marry	merry
Barry	berry (bury)

Other Spellings and/or Sounds

s

s	c				
assent	ascent			*Miscellaneous*	
sell	cell				
sent	cent(scent)				
site	cite(sight)				
serial	cereal				
counsel	council				
mussel	muscle				

air	heir	fir	fur	pray	prey
altar	alter	grate	great	root	route
ant	aunt	hay	hey	stake	steak
ark	arc	hairy	Harry	stayed	staid
base	bass	herd	heard	sun	son
bin	been	holy	wholly	surf	serf
brake	break	I	eye(aye)	surge	serge
bridal	bridle	I'll	aisle	their	there
brood	brewed	in	inn	too	two(to)
but	butt	idle	idol	urn	earn
by	buy(bye)	lesson	lessen	won	one
dual	duel	past	passed	worn	warn
faint	feint	paws	pause	yule	you'll

B. Some examples of words that are spelled the same but are pronounced differently because they have different meanings.

Vowel Sound

Short	*Long*		*Short*	*Long*		ō	ow
lead	lead		present	present		bow	bow
read	read		refuse	refuse		row	row
tear	tear		live	live		sow	sow
desert	desert		wind	wind			

		oo	ow
		wound	wound

REVIEW OF SOUNDS FOR TWO LETTER SPELLINGS *ch, ph, gh, qu.*

Assuming it has been postponed until now, this is a convenient place to review and explain further to the child the letter-sound relations of *ch*, *ph*, *gh*, and *qu*.

A. Remind him that there are two sounds we most often say for the letters *ch*.

1. Review and explain that usually when we see the letters *ch* together in a word we say the sound **ch**, as in *ch*op.

ch

ch . . .		. . *ch* . .	. . . *ch*	
chat	champ	anchovy	ranch	which
chap	channel	bachelor	bench	catch
chip	chess	enchant	cinch	perch
chug	chill	merchant	pinch	touch
chest	chapter	orchard	bunch	arch
chump	charge	purchase	lunch	detach

2. But that sometimes when we see the letters *ch* together at the *beginning* or *inside* a word we say the sound **k**, as in *ch*emist and me*ch*anic. Our *rule* is that if the word doesn't make sense when we say the sound **ch**, and it is a "big" word, then we *usually* say the sound **k**.

k

ch . . .		. . *ch* . .		
chameleon	Christ	ache	orchid	
chasm	choir	anchor	orchestra	
character	chord	architect	scheme	
chaos	chorus	bronchitis	schedule	
chemist	chrome	echo	school	
chronic	Christmas	mechanic	technical	

a. Point out that when we say **k** for the letters *ch* some words still won't make sense. Tell him that such words are exceptions. And that when we see the letters *ch* together in these words we usually say the sound **sh**, as in *Ch*icago.

sh

ch . . .		*. . ch . .*
Chicago	charade	mustache
champaign	chiffon	echelon
chaperone	chauffeur	machine

B. Remind him that we most often say one sound for the letters *ph*.

1. Review and explain that usually when we see the letters *ph* together in a word we say the sound **f**, as in *ph*one. Point out that the letters *ph* most often occur together at the *beginning* or *inside* a word.

f

ph . . .			*. . ph . .*		
phase	photo	Philip	alphabet	emphasis	Randolph
phrase	photograph	Philadelphia	asphalt	nephew	siphon
phantom	phone	philosopher	blasphemy	orphan	sophomore
pharmacy	phono	physical	catastrophe	pamphlet	sphere
pheasant	phonograph	physique	decipher	prophet	trophy
phenomenon	phony	Phoenix	elephant	Ralph	triumph

C. Remind him that he already knows that most often we say no sound for the letters *gh*.

1. Review and explain that usually when we see the letters *gh* together *inside* or at the *end* of a word the letters *gh* are "silent."

"Silent"

. . gh .	*. . . gh*
light	high
night	sigh
sight	thigh
eight	dough
weight	though

2. And that when we see the letters *gh* together at the *beginning* of a word we say the sound **g**, as in *gh*ost. (You can point out that there are only a few words that begin with the letters *gh*.)

g

gh . . .

ghastly
ghetto
ghost
ghoul

3. Then explain that for a few "crazy" words when we see the letters *gh* together at the *end* we say the sound **f**. Tell him that these are "crazy" words because they are exceptions.

f

. . . *gh*

enough	laugh
rough	cough
tough	trough
slough	

D. Remind him that we most often say one sound for the letters *qu*.

1. Review and explain that usually when we see the letters *qu* together in a word we say the sound **kw**, as in *qu*it. (Remind him also that when we see a letter *a* after the letters *qu* or *squ* we usually say a short sound **o** for the letter *a*.)

qu(+) . .

+ Short Sound Vowel			+ Long Sound Vowel	
quack	quick	quit	quaint	quiet
quell	quill	quiver	quake	quite
quench	quilt	quiz	quaver	quote
query	quip	quad (**o**)	queasy	quart (**ō**)
quest	quirk	quality	queen	quarter
quibble	quisling	quantity	queer	quarrel

REVIEW OF SOUNDS FOR TWO LETTER SPELLINGS **ch, ph, gh, qu.**   75

.. qu(+) ..

+ Short Sound Vowel			+ Long Sound Vowel	
aquarium	conquest	equivalent	liquor	acquaint
banquet	request	inquisitive	masquerade	equator
consequence	equip	vanquish	equal	marquee
sequence	liquid	aqualung (**u**)	equally	acquire
delinquent	sequin	adequate	sequel	require
frequent	equipment	conquer	tranquil	inquiry

squ(+) ..

+ Short Sound Vowel			+ Long Sound Vowel
squelch	squirrel	squalor	squeak
square	squirt	squander	squeal
squib	squab (**o**)	squash	squeamish
squid	squabble	squat	squeegee
squint	squad	squaw	squeeze
squirm	squall	squawk	squire

SOME *REGULAR* LETTER—SOUND COMBINATIONS at *Beginning* and *End* of Words

Some of the more frequent letter-sound combinations which occur at the beginning or end of words (i.e., prefixes and suffixes) are presented in this and the following section. The combinations presented in this section involve letter-sound relations which are regular or otherwise consistent with what has been covered already. The purpose here is to present these letter-sound combinations to the child as *units* which frequently occur at the beginning or end of words. If he has mastered the letter-sound correspondences covered so far, he should have little difficulty with the combinations presented in this section.

A.   Letter Combinations at *End* of Word: *One Sound*

Tell him that we say one sound for each of the following letter combinations, and that the vowel sound in each is short.

1.   Point out that when we see the letters *ment* together at the *end* of a word we say the sound **ment**, as in tor*ment*.

. . . ment

cement	argument	excitement
moment	apartment	experiment
garment	basement	instrument
torment	document	investment
fragment	compliment	judgment

2.   Point out that when we see the letters *ness* together at the *end* of a word we say the sound **nes**, as in happi*ness*.

. . . ness

madness	blindness	weakness
sadness	newness	happiness
dampness	poorness	cockiness
darkness	foolishness	clumsiness
sickness	awkwardness	silliness

B. Letter Combinations at *Beginning* of Word: *One Sound*

Tell him that we most often say one sound for each of the following letter combinations, and that the vowel sound in each is short.

1. Point out that when we see the letters *dis* together at the *beginning* of a word we usually say the sound **dis**, as in *dis*like.

dis . . .

disagree	discover	dislike	display	distinct
disappear	discuss	dismay	disposal	distinguish
disaster	disgrace	dismiss	disregard	distract
discard	disguise	disobey	disrupt	distress
discourage	disgust	disorder	distance	disturb

2. Point out that when we see the letters *en* together at the *beginning* of a word we usually say the sound **en**, as in *en*ter.

en . . .

enchant	energy	engulf	enroll	entrance
encourage	engaged	enjoy	entail	entry
endanger	engine	enlarge	enter	envy
endurance	engineer	enlist	entertain	envelope
enemy	engrave	enrich	entire	environment

3. Point out that when we see the letters *ex* together at the *beginning* of a word we usually say the sound **eks**, as in *ex*act.

ex . . .

exam	except	exercise	expect	explore
exact	excess	exert	expel	expose
exult	exchange	exile	expense	express
example	excite	exist	expert	extend
exceed	exclaim	exit	expire	extinct
excel	excuse	exotic	explain	extra
excellent	execute	expand	explode	extreme

4. Point out that when we see the letters *im* together at the *beginning* of a word we usually say the sound **im**, as in *im*pact.

im . . .

imitate	impersonate	impostor
impact	implant	impress
impair	implement	improper
impede	imply	improve
imperil	important	impulse

5. Point out that when we see the letters *in* together at the *beginning* of a word we usually say the sound **in**, as in *in*side.

in . . .

include	into	influence	inside	interest
income	infant	inform	insist	interfere
increase	infantry	injury	inspect	interrupt
indeed	infect	innocent	instant	introduce
index	inferior	inning	instead	invade
Indian	infield	insane	insult	invent
indicate	inflate	insect	instructor	invite

6. Point out that when we see the letters *un* together at the *beginning* of a word we usually say the sound **un**, as in *un*der.

un . . .

uncle	uneasy	underneath	unhurt	unreal
under	uneven	understand	unload	unseen
until	unfold	undress	unlikely	unsound
unless	unbend	unfasten	unnatural	untrue
undue	uncertain	unhappy	unpack	unused
unfit	uncover	unkind	unpaid	unwind

7. Point out that when we see the letters *sub* together at the *beginning* of a word we usually say the sound **sub**, as in *sub*merge.

sub . . .

submerge	substance	suburb
submarine	subgroup	submit
substitute	sublime	sublet
subtract	subside	subdue
subject	subscribe	subway

8. Point out that when we see the letters *trans* together at the *beginning* of a word we usually say the sound **trans**, as in *trans*fer.

trans . . .

transfer	translate
transistor	transmit
transport	transform
transplant	transit
transmission	transcirbe

C. Letter Combinations at *Beginning* of Word: *Two Sounds*

Tell him that because we say two different vowel sounds for the vowel letter we say two sounds for each of the following letter combinations.

1. Point out that when we see the letters *co* together at the *beginning* of a word we usually say either a short sound **o** or a long sound **ō** for the letter *o*.

    a. Explain that usually when we see the letters *co* together at the beginning of a word we first say the sound **ko**, as in *co*ffee.

ko

cobble	collar	copy
coffee	college	cosmic
cocky	collie	cotton
colony	Colorado	costume

    b. But if the word doesn't make sense then we usually say the sound **kō**, as in *co*coa.

kō

cocoa	Coca Cola	copilot
coed	collect	coral
cobra	Columbus	correct

2. Point out that when we see the letters *com* together at the *beginning* of a word we usually say either a short sound **o** or a short sound **u** for the letter *o*.

a. Explain that usually when we see the letters *com* together at the beginning of a word we first say the sound **kom**, as in *com*ic.

kom

combat	common	compliment
comedy	compact	compound
comic	competent	comprehend
comet	complex	comrade
comment	complicate	compensate

b. But if the word doesn't make sense then we usually say the sound **kum**, as in *com*pare. Explain also that we say both **kom** and **kum** for a few words, even though they are spelled the same, because they are different words having different meanings (Examples are in parentheses).

kum

(combat)	company	comply
(combine)	compare	component
comedian	compete	compose
complaint	complete	(compress)
comfort	(complex)	compute

(1) Point out that *often* when the letters *co* are followed by the double letter *m* we say a **ku** sound separately for the letters *co*.

co mmand	co mmute
co mmend	co mmunicate
co mmence	co mmunity
co mmodity	co mmittee

3. Point out that when we see the letters *con* together at the *beginning* of a word we also usually say either a short sound **o** or a short sound **u** for the letter *o*.

a. Explain that usually when we see the letters *con* together at the beginning of a word we first say the sound **kon**, as in *con*tact.

kon

con	contact	concentrate	confident	Congo
concept	congress	conference	confidence	conscious
concert	conquer	condescend	confiscate	contradict
concoct	conquest	consequence	congregate	contraband
concrete	convoy	constant	consolation	controversy

b. But if the word doesn't make sense then we usually say the sound **kun**, as in *con*cern.

kun

conceal	confess	confuse	control	contribute
conceit	confetti	congest	contempt	convenient
conceive	confine	connect	contain	consistent
concern	confirm	consent	convey	continue
conclude	conform	consider	convince	congratulate

c. Point out that we say both **kon** and **kun** for some words, even though they are spelled the same, because they are different words with different meanings.

kon and **kun**

conduct	contract
conflict	contrary
confound	contrast
content	convert
contest	convict

4. Point out that when we see the letters *di* together at the *beginning* of a word we usually say either a short sound **i** or a long sound **ī** for the letter *i*.

a. Explain that usually when we see the letters *di* together at the beginning of a word we first say the sound **di**, as in *di*ffer.

di

ditch	dimple	difficult	diminish
ditto	diploma	difference	divine
digit	dignity	diffuse	divot
divide	dignified	diversify	dizzy
divorce	dilemma	diligence	dilapidated

b.   But if the word doesn't make sense then we usually say the sound **dī**, as in *dī*et.

dī

dial	Diana	digest
dialect	diaper	dilate
diabetes	diver	dilute
diagram	diary	diagnose
diamond	diet	dinosaur

5.   Point out that when we see the letters *par* together at the *beginning* of a word we usually say either a short sound **o** or a short sound **e** for the letter *a*.

a.   Explain that usually when we see the letters *par* together at the beginning of a word we first say the sound **por**, as in *par*ka.

por

par	pardon	parking	party
parcel	parley	parlance	parted
parch	parson	partake	parting
parka	parsley	particle	participant
parlor	parsnip	partisan	parliament

b.   But if the word doesn't make sense then we usually say the sound **per**, as in *par*ent.

per

parent	parallel
Paris	paralyze
parish	paradise
parrot	paraffin
parakeet	paragraph

6.   Point out that when we see the letters *per* together at the *beginning* of a word we usually say either a short sound **u** or a short sound **e** for the letter *e*.

a. Explain that usually when we see the letters *per* together at the beginning of a word we first say the sound **pur**, as in *per*fect.

pur

perch	person	pertain	permanent
perky	percent	perjury	perpetuate
perfect	persist	persuade	persecute
perform	permit	percolate	pertinent
perfume	perhaps	pervade	perceive

b. But if the word doesn't make sense then we usually say the sound **per**, as in *per*ish.

per

Perry
perish
perilous
periscope

7. Point out that when we see the letters *pos* together at the *beginning* of a word we usually say either a long sound **ō** or a short sound **o** for the letter *o*.

a. Explain that usually when we see the letters *pos* together at the beginning of a word we first say the sound **pōs**, as in *pos*t.

pōs

posy	postpone
poster	postal
position	postman
possess	post office

b. But if the word doesn't make sense then we usually say the sound **pos**, as in *pos*itive.

pos

posse
possible
posture
positive

D. Letter Combinations at *Beginning* of Word : *Three Sounds*

Tell him that because we say three different vowel sounds for the vowel letter we say three sounds for each of the following letter combinations.

1. Point out that when we see the letters *de* together at the *beginning* of a word we usually say a long sound **ē**, short sound **i**, or short sound **e** for the letter *e*.

a. Explain that usually when we see the letters *de* together at the beginning of a word we first say the sound **dē** or **di**, as in *de*mon and *de*cide. (Point out that when we say **di** it's as if we start to say **dē** but then say only the first part of the **ē** sound.) Explain that in most words we can say either **dē** or **di**, but that usually a word sounds more like the way we naturally say it if we say **di**.

dē or **di**

December	demand	destroy	decency	defroster
decide	depend	defy	detail	delicious
defend	demon	deny	detach	delinquent
defeat	deposit	defect	detour	deodorant
define	depress	decoy	descend	department
degree	deprive	declare	device	detective
delay	desire	degrade	demolish	detergent
deliver	describe	Detroit	develop	determined

b. If the word doesn't make sense when we say either the sound **dē** or **di** then we usually say the sound **de**, as in *de*cade.

de

decade	depth	despite	delicatessen
decorate	deputy	destiny	demonstrate
definite	decimal	designate	desperado
deficit	detonate	delegate	detriment
denim	deference	democrat	devil

2. Point out that when we see the letters *re* together at the *beginning* of a word we also usually say a long sound **ē**, short sound **i**, or short sound **e** for the letter *e*.

a. Explain that usually when we see the letters *re* together at the beginning of a word we first say the sound **rē**, as in *re*cent.

rē

react	recent	rerun	reunite	redirect
recap	reflex	region	retail	reinforce
recast	refill	reorder	rehash	reconsider
reborn	refuel	regal	reprint	reconstruct
rebuild	reopen	restate	rebound	reproduce

b. But then explain that for *many* words that begin with the letters *re* we say both the sound **rē** and the sound **ri**. Explain that a word sounds more natural sometimes if we say **ri**, and at other times if we say **rē**. Also, that we say both sounds for some words because, even though they are spelled the same, they are different words having different meanings. Point out that if we're not sure which sound to say, we say the sound **rē** first. If the word doesn't sound right, then we say **ri**.

rē or ri

recall	regret	recite	remark	request
record	reject	receptive	refer	require
recover	reflect	relate	relief	research
recruit	reform	relax	rely	result
reclaim	refresh	release	reply	retire
reduce	receive	remain	report	retard

return	regain	repay	revolver	reliable
refund	rejoice	repeat	renew	religion
refuse	rejoin	revenge	restrict	responsible
refine	remind	reverse	resume	recuperate
recline	repair	review	removal	refrigerator
regard	repaid	revolt	reward	remember

c. If the word doesn't make sense when we say either the sound **rē** or **ri** then we usually say the sound **re**, as in *re*bel.

re

recipe	regular	relish	resident
recognize	regulate	remedy	represent
recollect	register	renegade	rectangle
referee	relevant	reptile	restaurant
refugee	relative	rescue	recommend

3. Point out that when we see the letters *pre* together at the *beginning*

of a word we also usually say a long sound **ē**, short sound **i**, or short sound **e** for the letter *e*.

a. Explain that usually when we see the letters *pre* together at the beginning of a word we first say the sound **prē**, as in *pre*vious.

prē

premature	preview
premium	previous
predispose	predetermine
prehistoric	preschool

b. But then explain that for *many* words that begin with the letters *pre* we say both the sound **prē** and the sound **pri**. Point out that if we're not sure which sound to say, we say the sound **prē** first. If the word doesn't sound right, then we say **pri**.

prē or **pri**

precise	prepare	pretense
precede	preside	preserve
predict	presume	prevail
prefer	pretend	prevent

c. If the word doesn't make sense when we say either the sound **prē** or **pri** then we usually say the sound **pre**, as in *pre*cious.

pre

preference	president
pregnant	pressure
prejudice	prestige
presence	pretzel

4. Point out that when we see the letters *pro* together at the *beginning* of a word we usually say a short sound **o**, long sound **ō**, or short sound **u** for the letter *o*.

a. Explain that usually when we see the letters *pro* together at the beginning of a word we first say the sound **pro**, as in *pro*per.

pro

problem	probably	prosper	progress
product	process	prospector	project
profit	prophet	prosecute	prominent
promise	properly	prodigy	propaganda
pronto	property	proverb	Protestant

b. If the word doesn't make sense then we usually say the sound **prō**, as in *pro*gram.

prō

pro	pronoun
profile	proscribe
program	protocol
prohibit	protrude

c. But then explain that for a number of words that begin with the letters *pro* we say both the sound **prō** and the sound **pru**. Point out that if we're not sure which sound to say, we say the sound **prō** first. If the word doesn't sound right, then we say **pru**.

prō or **pru**

produce	propose	prolific	productive
protect	proceed	projector	proclaimed
protest	progress	profound	profuse
prolong	provoke	proposed	pronounce
promote	provide	professor	propeller

SOME *IRREGULAR* LETTER—SOUND COMBINATIONS *at* **End** *of Words*

The combinations covered in this section involve a number of *irregular* letter-sound relations. As you will see, however, many of these irregular letter-sound relations are quite *simple* and *consistent*. Most children are pleased to learn about these combinations since almost everyone learning to read has difficulty with some of them.

Tell the child that now he is going to find out about some other units at the end of words. And that when we see some of these units we say some sounds that he would probably never be able to guess because they are pretty strange.

A.   Letter Combinations at *End* of Word: *One Sound*

Tell him that we say one sound for each of the following letter combinations.

1.   Point out that when we see the letters *ible* together at the *end* of a word we usually say the sound **ubl**, as in sens*ible*.

. . . *ible*

possible	sensible
responsible	convertible
horrible	credible
addible	incredible
accessible	indelible

2.   Point out that when we see the letters *sure* together at the *end* of a word we usually say the sound **zhur**, as in mea*sure*.

. . . *sure*

measure	leisure
pleasure	exposure
treasure	disclosure

3. Point out that when we see the letters *ture* together at the *end* of a word we usually say the sound **chur**, as in lec*ture*.

. . . ture

capture	lecture	puncture
culture	picture	gesture
creature	mixture	fixture
future	pasture	furniture
nature	torture	signature

And that when we see the letters *tur* inside and/or towards the end of a word we also say **chur**.

. . tur

cultural

natural

maturity

saturate

4. Point out that when we see the letters *ial* together at the *end* of a word we usually say the sound **ēul**, as in bur*ial*.

. . ial

burial	material	editorial
jovial	bacterial	memorial
genial	congenial	ceremonial
menial	remedial	custodial
serial	colonial	industrial

5. Point out that when we see the letters *cial* together at the *end* of a word we usually say the sound **shul**, as in so*cial*.

. . . cial

facial	special	financial
racial	official	especially
social	artificial	commercial
crucial	beneficial	superficial

6. Point out that when we see the letters *tial* together at the *end* of a word we usually say the sound **shul** (or **chul**), as in poten*tial*.

...tial

potential	confidential	substantial
essential	circumstantial	influential
residential	preferential	inferential
sequential	celestial	consequential

7. Point out that when we see the letters *ous* together at the *end* of a word we usually say the sound **us**, as in fam*ous*.

...ous

famous	enormous	tremendous
nervous	fabulous	strenuous
jealous	marvelous	continuous
generous	vigorous	monotonous
numerous	courteous	ridiculous

8. Point out that when we see the letters *ious* together at the *end* of a word we usually say the sound **ēus**, as in dev*ious*.

...ious

devious	obvious	mysterious
curious	previous	delerious
furious	hilarious	glorious
various	tedious	studious
serious	envious	industrious

9. Point out that when we see the letters *cious* or *tious* together at the *end* of a word we usually say the sound **shus**, as in deli*cious* and cau*tious*.

...cious		...tious
conscious	delicious	cautious
gracious	ferocious	bumptious
luscious	atrocious	fictitious
precious	spacious	nutritious
vicious	suspicious	pretentious

10. Point out that when we see the letters *ence* together at the *end* of a word we usually say the sound **uns**, as in influ*ence*.

absence	conference	preference
silence	excellence	persistence
presence	influence	existence
reference	intelligence	negligence

11. Point out that when we see the letters *dence* together at the *end* of a word we usually say the sound **duns**, as in confi*dence*.

. . . *dence*

confidence	residence
coincidence	cadence
dependence	precedence
evidence	incidence

12. Point out that when we see the letters *sive* together at the *end* of a word we usually say the sound **siv**, as in expen*sive*.

. . . *sive*

massive	cohesive	impressive
passive	compressive	oppressive
abrasive	expressive	permissive
pervasive	expensive	obtrusive

13. Point out that when we see the letters *tive* together at the *end* of a word we usually say the sound **tiv**, as in ac*tive*.

. . . *tive*

active	negative	attractive
captive	relative	affirmative
motive	sensitive	destructive
native	deceptive	descriptive
positive	incentive	detective

14. Point out that when we see the letters *eau* together at the *end* of a word we usually say the sound **ō**, as in bur*eau*.

. . . *eau*

beau	plateau
bureau	tableau
chapeau	trousseau

15. Point out that when we see the letters *igh* or *ight* together at the *end* of a word we usually say the sound **ī** and **īt**, as in th*igh* and l*ight*. (Remind him that he already knows that when we see the letters *gh* together *inside* or at the *end* of a word we usually say no sound for them.)

. . *igh*	. . . *ight*		
high	fight	right	plight
nigh	light	sight	slight
sigh	might	tight	bright
thigh	night	flight	fright

16. Point out that when we see the letters *ough* together at the *end* of a word we usually say the sound **ō**, as in th*ough*.

. . . *ough*	
dough	borough
though	thorough
although	

Tell him that the word *through* is an exception. Also point out that besides saying the sound **f** for the letters *gh* at the end of the following "crazy" words, we say either a short sound **o** or **u** for the letters *ou*.

of		**uf**	
cough		enough	tough
trough		rough	slough

17. Point out that when we see the letters *ought* and *aught* together at the *end* of a word we usually say the sound **ot**, as in th*ought* and t*aught*.

. . *ought*		. . *aught*	
ought	fought	caught	daughter
bought	thought	taught	slaughter
sought	brought	haughty	onslaught
		naughty	distraught

18. Point out that when we see the letters *eigh* and *eight* together at the *end* of a word we usually say the sound ā and āt, as in w*eigh* and w*eight*.

.. *eigh*		.. *eight*
weigh	neighbor	eight
neigh	inveigh	weight
sleigh		freight

Tell him that the words *height* and *sleight* are exceptions and that we say the sound ī for the letters *ei* in these words.

B. Letter Combinations at *End* of Word: *Two Sounds*

Tell him that we say two sounds for each of the following letter combinations.

1. Point out that when we see the letters *able* together at the *end* of a word we usually say either the sound ābl or **ubl**.

a. Explain that when we see the letters *able* together at the end of a smaller word we usually say ā**bl**, as in t*able*.

ābl	
able	stable
cable	enable
fable	disable
table	unable

b. And that when we see the letters *able* together at the end of a bigger word we usually say **ubl**, as in cap*able*.

ubl		
capable	constable	excitable
durable	comfortable	reliable
probable	charitable	incurable
adorable	considerable	available

2. Point out that when we see the letters *ance* together at the *end* of a word we usually say either the sound **ans** or **uns**.

a.   Explain that usually when we see the letters *ance* together at the end of a word we first say the sound **ans**, as in d*ance*.

ans

dance	romance
chance	enhance
trance	(entrance)
prance	finance
advance	circumstance

b.   But if the word doesn't make sense then we say the sound **uns**, as in perform*ance*.

uns

balance	fragrance	allowance
distance	endurance	appliance
clearance	ignorance	importance
nuisance	performance	resemblance
(entrance)	substance	tolerance

3.   Point out that when we see the letters *tain* together at the *end* of a word we usually say either the sound **tān** or **tun**.

a.   Explain that usually when we see the letters *tain* together at the end of a word we first say the sound **tān**, as in con*tain*.

tān

attain	contain
detain	sustain
retain	maintain
obtain	ascertain
pertain	entertain

b.   But if the word doesn't make sense then we say the sound **tun**, as in cer*tain*.

tun

captain
certain
curtain
fountain
mountain

4. Point out that when we see the letters *sion* together at the *end* of a word we usually say either the sound **shun** or **zhun**.

    a. Explain that usually when we see the letters *sion* together at the end of a word we first say the sound **shun**, as in ten*sion*.

shun

mansion	admission	extension
mission	confession	possession
pension	concussion	submission
tension	discussion	transmission

    b. But if the word doesn't make sense then we say the sound **zhun**, as in vi*sion*.

zhun

vision	occasion	provision
division	collision	conversion
confusion	conclusion	protrusion
precision	excursion	television

5. Point out that when we see the letters *tion* together at the *end* of a word we usually say either the sound **shun** or **chun**.

    a. Explain that usually when we see the letters *tion* together at the end of a word we first say the sound **shun**, as in mo*tion*.

shun

nation	auction	emotion	attention	invention
ration	section	adoption	condition	position
lotion	fiction	addition	correction	protection
notion	station	ambition	definition	selection
action	caution	affection	education	gumption

    b. But if the word doesn't make sense then we say a sound more like **chun**, as in ques*tion*.

chun

question	(mention)
bastion	(intention)
congestion	(prevention)

6.   Point out that when we see the letters *ior* together at the *end* of a word we usually say either the sound **yur** or **ēur** (or **ēyur**).

a.   Explain that when we see the letters *ior* together at the end of a word after the letters *n* or *v* we usually say the sound **yur**, as in jun*ior* and behav*ior*.

yur

junior	savior
senior	behavior

b.   And that when we see the letters *ior* together at the end of a word after the letter *r* we usually say the sound **ēur** (or **ēyur**), as in infer*ior*. (Have the child say whichever of the two sounds **ēur** or **ēyur** is easier or more natural for him.)

ēur (or **ēyur**)

anterior	ulterior
inferior	warrior

C.   Letter Combinations at *End* of Word : *Three Sounds*

Tell him that we say three sounds for the following letter combinations.

1.   Point out that when we see the letters *ion* or *ian* together at the *end* of a word we usually say a sound that is like **un**, **yun**, or **ēun** (or **ēyun**).

a.   Remind him that when we see the letters *sion* or *tion* together at the end of a word we often say the sound **shun**. Then explain that when we see the letters *ion* or *ian* together at the end of a word and they are part of a combination that begins with the letters *gi, ci, si, shi,* or *ti* we usually say just the sound **un** for the letters *on* or *an*, as in le*gion*, musi*cian*, ten*sion*, cu*shion*, and mo*tion*. (Point out that the letter *i* is silent and we say the sound **j** for *gi* and the sound **sh** for *ci*, *si*, *shi*, and *ti*.)

un

...*ion*				...*ian*		
legion	fashion	tension	motion	theologian	magician	Prussian
region	cushion	mansion	action	Georgian	musician	Russian
religion	contagion	mission	caution	politician	physician	martian

b.   Explain that when we see the letters *ion* or *ian* together at the end of a word after the letters *l* (*l*) or *n* we usually say the sound **yun**, as in battal*ion* and Ital*ian*.

yun

...*ion*				...*ian*	
billion	pavilion	onion	companion	Australian	Romanian
million	battalion	union	dominion	Italian	Californian
trillion	stallion	opinion	minion	Brazilian	Arizonian
rebellion	medallion	bunion	champion	civilian	Virginian

c.   And that otherwise when we see the letters *ion* or *ian* together at the end of a word we usually say the sound **ēun** (or **ēyun**), as in accord*ion* and Ind*ian*. (Have the child say whichever of the two sounds **ēun** or **ēyun** is easier or more natural for him.)

ēun (or ēyun)

...*ion*	...*ian*		
accordion	custodian	barbarian	Arabian
criterion	comedian	equestrian	bohemian
oblivion	guardian	historian	pedestrian
scorpion	Indian	librarian	vegetarian

D.   Some *Miscellaneous* Letter Combinations at *End* of Words: *One*, *Two*, or *Three Sounds*

For the most part the miscellaneous letter combinations at the end of words covered in this subsection are supplementary. In some instances the irregular letter-sound relations involved already have been presented in a different way in the preceding subsections. In other instances the relations involved are consistent with those presented in earlier sections.

If a child has difficulty with a particular letter combination, however, it is usually helpful to present or review it with him in the way it is outlined here.

1. Point out that when we see the letters *eon* together at the *end* of a word we usually say either the sound **ēon** or **un**.

a. Explain that usually when we see the letters *eon* together at the end of a word we say the sound **ēon**, as in n*eon*.

ēon

eon	neon
Leon	peon

b. But when we see the letters *eon* together at the end of a word after the letters *g* or *ch* we say the sound **un**, as in pig*eon*.

un

pigeon	bludgeon
surgeon	burgeon
dungeon	luncheon

2. Point out that when we see the letters *ue* together at the *end* of a word we usually say the sound **o͞o** or **ū**, but that sometimes we say no sound at all.

a. Review and explain that usually when we see the letters *ue* together at the end of a word we first say the sound **o͞o**, as in s*ue*.

o͞o

due	clue	fondue
sue	blue	pursue
rue	glue	accrue
true	untrue	misconstrue

b. And that if the word doesn't make sense then we usually say the sound **ū**, as in resc*ue*.

ū

issue	cue	continue
tissue	rescue	argue
statue	venue	virtue

c. But then explain that usually when we see either the letters *gue* or *que* at the end of a word the letters *ue* are silent and we say just the sound **g** or **k**, as in va*gue* and anti*que*.

g			**k**	
. . . gue			*. . . que*	
vague	league	colleague	unique	plaque
vogue	morgue	catalogue	antique	brusque
rogue	tongue	monologue	clique	opaque
brogue	fatigue	travelogue	critique	burlesque
plague	intrigue	harangue	physique	grotesque

3. Point out that when we see the letters *ace*, *age*, or *ate* together at the *end* of a word we usually say a long **ā** or a short sound **i** (or **u**) for the letter *a*.

a. Review and explain that usually when we see the letter *a* followed by a consonant letter and a silent letter *e* at the end of a word we say a long sound **ā** for the letter *a*, as in f*ace*, c*age*, and d*ate*.

ā

. . . ace		*. . . age*		*. . . ate*	
face	trace	cage	engage	date	concentrate
race	grace	page	outrage	plate	fascinate
place	unlace	wage	enrage	skate	imitate
space	embrace	stage	rampage	alternate	regulate

b. But then explain that if the word doesn't sound right we usually then say a sound for the letter *a* that is more like a short sound **i** (or **u**), as in pal*ace*, garb*age*, and accur*ate*. (Have him say whichever of the two sounds **i** or **u** is easier or more natural for him.)

i (or u)

. . . ace		. . . age			. . . ate	
furnace	terrace	bandage	damage	manage	agate	desperate
menace	preface	cabbage	garbage	marriage	accurate	(deliberate)
palace	solace	cottage	hostage	package	adequate	(moderate)
necklace	populace	carriage	image	village	appropriate	Senate

(1) Point out that if a word still doesn't sound right when we say the sound ā or i for the letter a in *age* then we usually say a short sound o, as in gar*age*.

o

. . . age

garage	massage
mirage	camouflage
corsage	sabotage

4. Point out that when we see the letters *ice, ile, ine, ite,* or *ive* together at the *end* of a word we usually say a long sound ī or a short sound i for the letter *i*.

a. Review and explain that usually when we see the letter *i* followed by a consonant letter and a silent letter *e* at the end of a word we say a long sound ī for the letter i, as in n*ice,* f*ile,* f*ine,* b*ite,* and d*ive.*

ī

. . ice		. . . ile		. . . ine	
nice	price	file	reptile	fine	decline
vice	device	smile	compile	shine	canine
slice	twice	while	crocodile	confine	iodine
spice	entice	profile	juvenile	combine	turpentine

. . . ite		. . . ive	
bite	termite	dive	connive
spite	appetite	five	revive
polite	dynamite	strive	survive
ignite	satelite	arrive	contrive

b. But then explain that if the word doesn't sound right we usually then say a short sound i for the letter *i*, as in not*ice,* frag*ile,* eng*ine,* gran*ite,* and g*ive.*

i

. . ice		. . . ile		. . . ine	
notice	practice	fragile	imbecile	engine	medicine
justice	accomplice	fertile	(mobile)	examine	masculine
crevice	cowardice	futile	versatile	imagine	feminine
Venice	precipice	missile	volatile	genuine	margarine

. . . ite	. . . ive	
granite	give	river
opposite	(live)	liver
definite	olive	sliver
favorite	active	quiver

(1)   Point out that if a word still doesn't sound right when we say the sound ī or i for the letter *i* in *ine* then we usually say a long sound ē for the letter *i,* as in gaso*line*.

ē

. . . *ine*

marine	sardine	limousine
machine	morphine	figurine
gasoline	nectarine	quarantine
magazine	nicotine	tangerine

5.   Point out that when we see the letters *tu* together at the *end* of a word we usually say the sound **t** or **ch** for the letter *t*.

a.   Review and explain that when we see the letters *tu* together toward the end of a word and they are *followed* by a *consonant letter* we usually say the sound **t** for the letter *t* (And usually the sound o͞o for the letter *u*), as in as*tu*te.

t

astute	attitude
constitute	fortitude
institute	gratitude

b.   But that when we see the letters *tu* together toward the end of a word and they are *followed* by a *vowel letter* then we usually say the sound **ch** for the letter *t* (And usually the sound o͞o for the letter *u*), as in sta*tu*e.

ch

actuate	statue	actual	spiritual
situate	virtue	factual	tortuous
fluctuate	eventually	mutual	virtuous
accentuate	constituent	perpetual	sumptuous

(1) Remind him of the exception that when we see the letters *tur* inside or *ture* at the end of a word we also say the sound **ch** for the letter *t*.

chur		Additional Exceptions
capture	cultural	fortune
creature	natural	fortunate
future	maturity	capitulate
lecture	saturate	tarantula

6. Point out that when we see the letters *ti* together at the *end* of a word we usually say the sound **t**, **sh**, or **ch** for the letter *t*.

a. Review and explain that when we see the letters *ti* together toward the end of a word and they are *followed* by a *consonant letter* we usually say the sound **t** for the letter *t* (and usually a short sound **i** for the letter *i*), as in boun*ti*ful.

t

article	cultivate	constitute
bountiful	fortitude	particular
plentiful	gratitude	vertical

b. But that when we see the letters *ti* together toward the end of a word and they are *followed* by a *vowel letter* then we usually say the sound **sh** or **ch** for the letter *t* (and the letter *i* is silent), as in par*ti*al and ques*ti*on.

(1)   Explain that we first say the sound **sh**, as in par*ti*al.

sh

martian	cautious	patient	attention
martial	bumptious	quotient	condition
partial	fictitious	negotiable	correction
substantial	pretentious	station	position
confidential	nutritious	ambition	selection

(a)   Point out that when we see *tiate* at the end of a word we say a long sound **ē** for the letter *i*.

initiate
negotiate
potentiate
vitiate

(2)   But if the word doesn't sound right then we say a sound more like **ch**, as in ques*ti*on.

ch

potential	question	(mention)
essential	bastion	(prevention)
sequential	congestion	(intervention)

7.   Point out that often when we see the letters *ia*, *ie*, *io*, or *iu* together in a letter combination at the *end* of a word we say either the sound **ēu** or **u**. (Remind him that we say one of these sounds for the letters *ia* or *io* when we see *ial*, *ian*, *ion*, or *ior* at the end of a word.)

a.   Explain that when we see the letters *ia*, *ie*, *io*, or *iu* together in a letter combination at the end of a word we usually first say a long sound **ē** for the letter *i* and a short sound **u** for the letter *a*, *e*, *o*, or *u*, as in al*ia*s, al*ie*n, per*io*d, and gen*iu*s.

ēu

. . *ia* .				. . *ie* .			
burial	Indian	alias	malaria	barrier	Orient	twentieth	alien
genial	custodian	amiable	cafeteria	clothier	obedient	thirtieth	audience
jovial	comedian	lariat	criteria	furrier	salient	sixtieth	Gabriel
menial	librarian	anemia	euphoria	harrier	convenient	eightieth	Soviet

accordion	anterior	chariot	period	genius	medium	premium	chromium
criterion	inferior	idiot	axiom	Cassius	stadium	auditorium	uranium
oblivion	interior	patriot	idiom	Julius	opium	aquarium	moratorium
scorpion	ulterior	warrior	oriole	geranium	podium	gymnasium	sanitarium

(1)   Point out the exception that when we see just the letters io together at the end of a word then we usually say a long sound ō for the letter o, as in rad*io*.

ē ō

trio	radio	studio
patio	ratio	cheerio
polio	curio	pistachio

b.   But then explain that when we see the letters ia, ie, or io together at the end of a word and they are part of a letter combination which begins with gi, ci, si, shi, or ti we usually say just a short sound **u** for the letter a, e, or o which follows (The letter i is silent.), as in Geor*gia*, an*cie*nt, Rus*sia*, fa*shio*n, and mili*tia*. (Point out and remind him that we usually say the sound **j** for gi and the sound **sh** for ci, si, shi, and ti.)

u

. . ia .		. . ie .		. . io .	
Borgia	Russia	ancient	conscience	legion	prodigious
Georgia	amnesia	deficient	patience	region	delicious
inertia	magician	efficient	patient	religion	gracious
militia	musician	sufficient	quotient	contagious	cautious

(1)   Remind him that when we see the letters ian together at the end of a word after the letter l or n we usually say the sound **yun.** Then point out that when we see just the letters ia together at the end of a word after the letter l or n we usually say the sound **yu** (or **ēyu**), as in magnol*ia* and ammon*ia*.

yu (or ēyu)

. . . ia

Australia	ammonia
Brazilia	California
magnolia	petunia
dahlia	Virginia

SILENT CONSONANT LETTERS

Only silent *consonant* letters are considered in this section. The more important silent *vowel* letters already have been covered elsewhere in this outline. (Since other instances of silent *vowel* letters are relatively infrequent they can be dealt with by regarding them as exceptions and by teaching the words in which they occur as sight words.)

One good way to deal with silent letters is to have the child keep a chart of silent-letter words that he encounters in his reading. Then, after he has recorded three or four words involving a particular silent letter, possible cues can be pointed out to help him recognize and pronounce further instances.

Some children have little difficulty with the more common silent consonant letters. Some also find that by only partially or slightly saying a so-called silent consonant letter it is possible to recognize and correctly say a fairly large number of words.

A. Letter Combinations with One or More Letters Silent

1. Point out that when we see the letters *dge* together in a word the *d* is silent and we usually just say the sound **j**. Also point out that the letters *dge* usually occur toward or at the end of a word.

. . . dge

badge	pledge	dodge	nudge	badger	fidget	partridge
edge	sledge	lodge	sludge	ledger	midget	porridge
hedge	dredge	budge	smudge	Dodger	budget	dislodge
ledge	ridge	fudge	grudge	lodger	abridge	misjudge
wedge	bridge	judge	trudge	drudgery	cartridge	hodge podge

2. Point out that when a word begins with the letters *kn* the *k* is silent and we just say the sound **n**.

kn . . .

knack	kneel	knob
knave	knead	knock
knelt	knife	knot
knew	knight	know
knee	knit	knowledge

3. Point out that when a word begins or ends with the letters *gn* the *g* is silent and we just say the sound **n**.

gn . . .		*. . . gn*
gnash	sign	malign
gnat	align	feign
gnaw	assign	champagne
gnome	design	cologne
gnarled	benign	(poignant)

4   Review and point out that when we see the letters *gh* together inside or at the end of a word they are usually silent.

. . gh . .	*. . . gh*
daughter	high
neighbor	sigh
lightning	thigh
frightening	dough
thoughtful	though

5. Point out that when a word begins with the letters *wr* the *w* is silent and we just say the sound **r**. Remind him also that in a few words which begin with the letters *wh* the *w* is silent and we just say the sound **h**. (It may or may not be necessary to point out to a given child the silent *w* in the words *answer* and *sword*.)

wr . . .		*wh . . .*
wrap	wrist	who
wreck	written	whom
wrench	write	whose
wrinkle	wrong	whole
wring	wrote	wholly

6. Point out that when we see the letters *tch*, *stle*, *sten*, and sometimes *et*, together at the end of a word the letter *t* is silent. Then point out that the letter *t* also is silent when it occurs inside or at the end of a few other words.

. . tch	. . stle	. . sten	. . et	"Other"
catch	hustle	fasten	valet	depot
batch	rustle	listen	chalet	debut
witch	thistle	glisten	crochet	mortgage
watch	whistle	moisten	ricochet	Christmas
blotch	wrestle	christen	Chevrolet	

7. Point out that when we see the letters *mn* together at the end of a word the letter *n* is silent and we just say the sound **m**.

. . *mn*
hymn
condemn
solemn
column

B. Single Silent Letter

1. Point out that when the letter *b* is silent it is usually when it occurs at or toward the end of a word, and usually when it occurs at the end of a word after the letter *m* or before the letter *t*.

. . . *b*

lamb	climb	debt
limb	dumb	doubt
bomb	thumb	subtle

2. Point out that when the letter *h* is silent it is usually when it occurs at the beginning or inside a word.

h . . .

heiress	exhaust	John
honor	exhibit	rhythm
honest	dinghy	khaki
hour	dahlia	wharf

3. Point out that when the letter *l* is silent it is usually when it occurs toward the end or inside a word.

	. . *l* .		. . *l* . .
balk	calm	calf	salve
talk	palm	half	solder
walk	qualm	could	salmon
chalk	folk	would	Lincoln
stalk	yolk	should	

4. Point out that when the letter *p* is silent it is usually when it occurs at the beginning of a word and is followed by another consonant letter.

p . . .	
psalm	psychic
pshaw	psychology
pseudo	pneumonia

C. Some Words Pronounced the Same but Spelled Differently

The word pairs listed below can be used to review (or teach) various silent letters. They also can be intermixed with the word pairs listed in Section XVI, and then presented as a challenging game which provides a measure of a child's reading skills. [Note that the pairs listed do not exhaust the possibilities. You or the child may think of other pairs (or triplets)—you can add.]

lam	lamb	slay	sleigh	air	heir	yoke	yolk
plum	plumb	way	weigh	nose	knows	wood	would
rain	reign	ate	eight	not	knot	chock	chalk
cot	caught	wait	weight	night	knight	rap	wrap
taut	taught	threw	through	new	knew	ring	wring
sot	sought	bow	bough	no	know	rote	wrote
hi	high	doe	dough	Neil	kneel	right	write
mite	might	time	thyme	need	knead	rye	wry
write	right	cord	chord	coo	coup	hole	whole
strait	straight	our	hour	him	hymn	holy	wholly

XXI

SOME COMMON WORDS
AND SOME IRREGULAR WORDS

For your convenience, two groups of words have been listed here. Those in Section A are common words which can often be taught with profit, right from the start, as sight words. Many of them involve only regular sound and letter relations. Some involve an irregular relation. Taken together, the words listed account for from about 45 to 70 percent of all the words that are encountered in reading graded reading books in school, and in reading stories, advertisements, and articles in newspapers and magazines. Simply mastering these words, therefore, can have a marked effect on reading skill.

The words listed in Section B involve various irregularities in sound and letter relations. On the whole, the inconsistencies involved are not covered by sound and letter relations presented in preceding parts of the manual. Some of the words listed are fairly common ones, and they can be taught on a sight basis and/or as exceptions when they are encountered.

A.   List of Common Words

In looking over the words listed in this subsection you will see why many of them are often difficult to master. Some of them have both a similar spelling and pronunciation. Others have a similar spelling but different pronunciation or a similar pronunciation but different spelling. In order to minimize these points of confusion, it's usually a good idea to present only four or five of these words at a time and then to stay with them until they are mastered. Once they can be read at a glance, then four or five others can be presented, and so on.

a
about
after
again
ago
am
among
an
and
any
are
aren't
as
at
away

be
been
big
bit
bite
black
both
but
by

came
cold
come
could

did
didn't
do
does
doesn't
done
don't
down

each
early
easy
even
ever
every

fall
fell
fill
find
first
for
found
four
from
full

get
give
go
goes
gone
grow

had
hadn't
has
hasn't
have
he
he'll
her
here
him
his
how

I
I'll
if
I'm
in
into
is
isn't
it

kind
know

laugh
led
let
let's
live

many
may
me
more
move
much
must
my

new
no
none
not
now

of
off
often
on
once
one
only
open
or
other
our
out
over
own

put

quit
quiet
quite

said
saw
say
says
see
she
she'll
should
show
so
some
soon
sure

tall
tell
that
the
their
them
then
there
these
they
they're
this
those
though
three
through
to
too
two

up
upon
us
use

very
view

wait
walk
wall
want
warm
was
wasn't
we
we'll
well
went
were
we're
weren't
what
when
where
who
whose
why
with
would

yes
yet
you
you'll
your
you're

B. List of Irregular Words

The list of words in this subsection is not exhaustive, and other words can be added as you bump into them.

adieu	cafe	hallelujah	people	sieve
aeon	canoe	heart	phoenix	ski
aerial	caprice	hearth	plaid	sleight
aesthetic	colonel	height	police	sorghum
aisle	coyote	idea	porpoise	soldier
barbeque	door	iron	promise	stein
beauty	Europe	kayak	prove	sugar
blood	flood	language	push	theory
broad	floor	leopard	quay	tomb
bury	foetid	liquor	recipe	wolf
business	friend	maestro	rendezvous	women
busy	gauge	minute	sergeant	Xenophon
buy	guest	ocean	sew	yacht
caesarian	guy	parliament	shoe	yeoman

Expanded Lists of Words: Consonant Letter-Sound Combinations with Single Short Vowel Sounds at the *End* of Words [See pages 19–23]

Two Letters

ab	ib	ob	ub	at	et	it	ot	ut
cab	bib	bob	hub	bat	bet	bit	bot	but
dab	fib	cob	cub	cat	get	fit	cot	cut
Fab	jib	dob	dub	fat	jet	hit	dot	gut
gab	rib	fob	hub	gat	let	kit	got	hut
jab	sib	gob	nub	hat	met	lit	hot	jut
lab	glib	job	pub	mat	net	pit	jot	nut
nab	crib	lob	rub	nat	pet	quit	lot	rut
tab	squib	mob	sub	pat	set	sit	not	glut
blab		nob	tub	rat	vet	wit	pot	smut
flab		rob	club	sat	wet	flit	rot	shut
slab		sob	flub	vat	yet	slit	sot	strut
crab		blob	glub	flat	fret	whit	tot	
drab		glob	drub	plat	whet	grit	blot	
grab		slob	grub	slat	Chet	skit	clot	
scab		snob	snub	brat		spit	plot	
stab		swob	stub	drat		twit	slot	
		thob	scrub	frat		exit	trot	
		throb	shrub	scat		split	snot	
			chub	spat			shot	
				splat			spot	
				that				
				chat				

ap	ip	op	up	ad	ed	id	od	ud
cap	dip	bop	cup	bad	bed	bid	cod	bud
gap	hip	cop	pup	cad	fed	did	God	cud
jap	lip	hop	sup	dad	led	hid	hod	dud

Continued on following page.

ap	ip	op
lap	nip	lop
map	pip	mop
nap	quip	pop
rap	rip	sop
sap	sip	top
tap	tip	clop
yap	yip	flop
zap	zip	glop
clap	blip	plop
flap	clip	slop
slap	flip	crop
crap	ship	drop
trap	drip	prop
snap	grip	shop
scrap	trip	stop
strap	skip	chop
chap	snip	strop
	ship	
	strip	
	whip	
	chip	

ad	ed	id	od	ud
fad	Ned	kid	mod	Hud
gad	red	lid	nod	mud
had	Ted	quid	pod	Pud
lad	wed	rid	rod	crud
mad	Zed	slid	sod	spud
pad	bled	grid	clod	
sad	fled	skid	plod	
clad	sled	squid	prod	
glad	dred		trod	
brad	Fred		shod	
grad	shed			
Thad	shred			
Chad	spred			

ax	ex	ox	ix, ux	ag	eg	ig	og	ug
ax	hex	box	fix	bag	beg	big	bog	bug
lax	Rex	fox	mix	hag	keg	dig	dog	dug
sax	sex	lox	six	jag	leg	fig	fog	hug
tax	vex	pox	lux	lag	Meg	gig	hog	jug
wax	flex	sox	tux	nag	peg	jig	jog	lug
flax	Chex		flux	rag	Greg	Mig	log	mug
			crux	sag		pig	clog	pug
				tag		rig	flog	rug
				wag		wig	frog	tug
				zag		zig	grog	slug
				flag		brig	smog	drug
				slag		prig		smug
				brag		swig		snug
				crag		twig		shrug
				drag		whig		thug
				snag		sprig		chug
				shag				
				stag				
				swag				

am	im	um	em, om		an	en	in	on, un
am	dim	bum	gem		an	Ben	bin	con
bam	him	gum	hem		ban	den	din	Don
cam	Jim	hum	Lem		can	hen	fin	Jon
dam	Kim	Lum	Mom		Dan	Ken	gin	Lon
gam	rim	rum	Tom		fan	Len	kin	Ron
ham	Tim	sum	prom		Jan	men	pin	bun
jam	slim	yum			man	pen	sin	dun
lam	brim	glum			Nan	ten	tin	fun
Pam	grim	plum			pan	yen	win	gun
ram	prim	slum			ran	zen	grin	nun
Sam	trim	drum			tan	glen	skin	pun
yam	skim	scum			van	then	spin	run
blam	swim	strum			clan	when	twin	sun
clam	whim	chum			plan		thin	shun
Fram					bran		chin	spun
gram					Fran			stun
pram					scan			
sham					span			
Spam					Stan			
swam					Chan			
exam								
scram								
wham								

Three Letters

ang	ing	ong	ung		ank	ink	onk, unk
bang	bing	bong	dung		bank	ink	honk
dang	king	Fong	gung		dank	fink	konk
gang	Ming	gong	hung		Hank	kink	bunk
hang	ping	Kong	lung		rank	link	dunk
rang	ring	long	rung		sank	mink	gunk
sang	sing	pong	sung		tank	pink	junk
Tang	wing	song	clung		yank	rink	lunk
clang	zing	strong	flung		blank	sink	punk
slang	cling		slung		clank	wink	sunk
whang	fling		swung		flank	blink	clunk
sprang	sling		stung		plank	clink	flunk
chang	bring		sprung		crank	plink	plunk
	sting		strung		drank	slink	slunk
	spring		chung		frank	brink	drunk
	string				prank	crink	trunk
	thing				shank	drink	skunk
					spank	stink	spunk
					stank	shrink	stunk
					swank	think	shrunk
					shrank	chink	chunk

ant	ent	int	ont, unt		and	end	ond
ant	bent	hint	font		band	bend	bond
can't	cent	lint	bunt		hand	fend	fond
pant	dent	mint	hunt		land	lend	pond
rant	gent	tint	punt		sand	mend	blond
plant	Kent	flint	runt		bland	send	
slant	lent	glint	blunt		gland	tend	
grant	pent	print	brunt		brand	vend	
scant	rent	stint	grunt		grand	wend	
chant	sent	splint	shunt		spand	blend	
	tent	sprint	stunt		stand	spend	
	vent	squint			strand	trend	
	went						
	scent						
	spent						

ell	ill	oll	ull		ash	ush	esh, ish, osh
bell	bill	doll	bull		ash	gush	mesh
cell	dill	loll	cull		bash	hush	flesh
fell	hill	moll	dull		dash	lush	fresh
jell	kill		full		cash	mush	thresh
quell	mill		gull		gash	rush	dish
sell	pill		hull		hash	blush	fish
tell	quill		lull		lash	flush	wish
well	rill		mull		mash	plush	swish
Prell	sill		null		rash	slush	squish
smell	till		pull		clash	brush	gosh
spell	will		skull		flash	crush	posh
swell	drill				slash	thrush	slosh
shell	frill				brash		Frosh
yell	grill				crash		
	trill				trash		
	skill				smash		
	spill				splash		
	still				stash		
	swill				thrash		
	shrill						
	thrill						
	chill						

ack	eck	ick	ock	uck	amp	ump	emp, omp, imp
back	Beck	Dick	dock	duck	camp	bump	hemp
hack	deck	kick	jock	luck	damp	dump	pomp
jack	heck	lick	hock	muck	lamp	hump	romp
lack	neck	nick	lock	puck	ramp	lump	clomp
pack	peck	pick	pock	suck	tamp	mump	tromp
quack	fleck	quick	rock	tuck	vamp	pump	stomp
rack	check	sick	sock	cluck	clamp	rump	chomp
sack	speck	tick	block	pluck	cramp	sump	limp
tack		wick	clock	truck	tramp	clump	blimp
black		click	flock	snuck	scamp	plump	crimp
flack		chick	crock	shuck	stamp	slump	skimp
slack		flick	shock	struck	champ	grump	primp
crack		slick	stock	chuck		trump	scrimp
track		brick	chock			stump	shrimp
smack		crick				whump	chimp
snack		prick				thump	
shack		trick				chump	
stack		stick					
swack		thick					
whack							

ast	est	ist	ust	ost	aft	ift	uft, oft, eft
cast	best	fist	bust	cost	daft	gift	tuft
fast	jest	gist	dust	lost	raft	lift	loft
last	nest	list	gust	frost	Taft	rift	soft
mast	pest	mist	just		waft	sift	deft
past	rest	twist	lust		craft	drift	heft
vast	test	exist	must		draft	shift	left
blast	vest	grist	rust		graft	swift	theft
	west		crust		shaft	thrift	
	zest		trust		chaft		
	chest						
	crest						
	quest						

atch	itch	etch	otch	utch
batch	itch	fetch	botch	Dutch
catch	ditch	sketch	blotch	hutch
hatch	hitch	stretch	crotch	clutch
latch	Mitch	wretch	scotch	crutch
match	pitch		splotch	
patch	witch			
snatch	britches			
thatch	snitch			
scratch	switch			
	twitch			
	which			

Additional Three *Letter* (*Vowel Letter* +)

+ *lt*			+ *ct*			+ *pt*		+ *lf*
belt	hilt	cult	act	strict		apt	script	elf
felt	jilt		fact	duct		rapt		self
melt	kilt		pact			kept		golf
pelt	lilt		tact			wept		gulf
welt	quilt		tract			strept		shelf
whelt	silt		exact					
	tilt							
	wilt							
	stilt							
	spilt							

+ *lk*		+ *lm*	+ *lp*	+ *sk*		+ *sp*	
elk	bulk	elm	help	ask	desk	asp	lisp
ilk	hulk	helm	kelp	bask	risk	gasp	wisp
bilk	sulk	film	gulp	cask	dusk	rasp	
milk			pulp	mask	husk	clasp	
silk			scalp	task	tusk	grasp	
				flask			
				brisk			
				frisk			
				whisk			

Expanded Lists of Words Arranged By Common *Beginning*: Consonant Letter-Sound Combinations with Single Short Vowel Sounds [See pages 23–24]

bl		*cl*			*fl*				*gl*		
blab	blob	clack	click	clock	flack	fleck	flick	flock	glib	glob	glub
black	block	clang	cling	clung	flash	flesh	flush		glad		
bland	blend	clap	clip	clop	flap	flip	flop		gland		
blank	blink	clad	clod		flax	flex	flux		glen		
blam		clamp	clump		flab	flub			glint		
blast		clam			flag	flog			glop		
bled		clan			flank	flunk			glug		
blip		clash			flat	flit			glum		
blimp		clasp			fling	flung			glut		
blot		cleft			flask						
blond		clog			fled						
blush		clot			flint						
		club									
		cluck									
		clutch									

pl			*sl*			*br*		*cr*		
plank	plink	plunk	slam	slim	slum	brad	bred	crack	crick	crock
plat	plot		slang	sling	slung	brag	brig	cramp	crimp	
plan			slap	slip	slop	brash	brush	crap	crop	
plant			slash	slush	slosh	Breck	brick	crash	crush	
plod			slat	slit	slot-	Brent	brunt	crest	crust	
plop			slack	slick		bring	brung	crotch	crutch	
plug			slab	slob		brisk	brusk	crab		
pluck			sled	slid		bran		craft		

Continued on following page.

pl	*sl*	*br*	*cr*
plum	slant	brand	crag
plump	slept	brat	cram
	slug	brim	crank
	slump	brink	crept
			crisp
			crud

dr			*fr*		*gr*		*pr*			*tr*		
drank	drink	drunk	frat	fret	grab	grub	pram	prim	prom	track	trick	truck
drab	drub		Fran		grad	grid	prank			tramp	tromp	trump
draft	drift		frank		gram	grim	Prell			tram	trim	
drag	drug		Fram		gramp	grump	prick			trap	trip	
dram	drum		Fred		grant	grunt	prig			tred	trod	
drill	droll		fresh		graft		primp			tract		
drip	drop		frill		grand		print			trash		
drat			frisk		grasp		prod			trend		
dred			frock		grin		prop			trill		
			frost		grip					trot		
					grist					trunk		
					grit					trust		
					grog							

sc	*sk*		*sm*		*sn*		*sp*		
scab	skill	skull	smack	smock	snack	snuck	span	spin	spun
scamp	sketch		smash		snag	snug	spat	spit	spot
scan	skid		smell		snap	snip	spank	spunk	
scant	skim		smelt		snatch	snitch	sped	spud	
scat	skimp		smut		snob	snub	spell	spill	
scent	skin				snit	snot	spelt	spilt	
scum	skip						Spam		
	skit						speck		
	skunk						spend		
							spent		

st				*sw*			*ch*			
stack	stick	stock	stuck	swam	swim	swum	champ	chimp	chomp	chump
stamp	stomp	stump		swang	swing	swung	check	chick	chock	chuck
stab	stub			swag	swig		chap	chip	chop	
Stan	stun			swell	swill		chat	chit		
sting	stung			swank			chink	chunk		
stink	stunk			swept			chub	chug		
stint	stunt			swift			chaft			

st	*sw*	*ch*
stag	swish	chant
stand	switch	chest
stash		Chex
stat		chill
stem		chin
still		chum
stilt		
stitch		
stop		
stuck		

sh			*th*		*wh*		*ex*	*qu*		*tw*
shack	Shick	shock	("Hard")		wham	whim	exact	quack	quick	twang
shaft	shift		thank	think	whet	whit	exam	quaft		twig
shed	shod		thing	thong	whip	whop	exit	quest		twill
shin	shun		thatch		whack		exist	quid		twin
ship	shop		thett		whelm		exalt	quill		twist
shot	shut		thick		whelp		exult	quilt		twit
shag			thin		whelt			quip		twitch
shank			thud		when			quit		
shell			thug		whisk					
			thump							
			("Soft")							
			than							
			that							
			them							
			then							

REFERENCES

ENGELMANN, SIEGFRIED, and THERESE ENGELMANN, *Give Your Child a Superior Mind*, New York: Simon and Schuster, 1966.

HALL, ROBERT A., JR., *Sound and Spelling in English*. Philadelphia: Chilton Co., 1961.

SOFFIETTI, JAMES P., "Why Children Fail to Read: a Linguistic Analysis," *Harvard Educational Review*, 25, (1955), 63–84.

THORNDIKE, E. L., and CLARENCE L. BARNHART, *High School Dictionary*. Chicago, Ill.: Scott, Foresman Co., 1965.

TRAGER, GEORGE L., and HENRY LEE SMITH, JR., *Outline of English Structure*. Norman, Okla.: Battenburg Press, 1951.